Not Bosses
But
Leaders

How to lead the way to success

3rd edition

JOHN ADAIR

**KOGAN
PAGE**

London and Philadelphia

Publisher's note

Every possible effort has been made to ensure that the information contained in this book is accurate at the time of going to press, and the publishers and author cannot accept responsibility for any errors or omissions, however caused. No responsibility for loss or damage occasioned to any person acting, or refraining from action, as a result of the material in this publication can be accepted by the editor, the publisher or the author.

First published in 1987 by the Talbot Adair Press, Westbury Manor, Compton, Guildford GU3 1EE
Second edition 1990
Revised second edition 1997
Third edition 2003
Reprinted 2003
Paperback edition 2006
Reprinted 2006, 2007, 2008
This edition 2009
Reprinted 2009

Kogan Page Limited
120 Pentonville Road
London N1 9JN
United Kingdom
www.koganpage.com

Kogan Page US
525 South 4th Street, #241
Philadelphia PA 19147
USA

ISBN   978 0 7494 5481 4

British Library Cataloguing-in-Publication Data

A CIP record for this book is available from the British Library.

Library of Congress Cataloging-in-Publication Data

Adair, John Eric, 1934-
   Not bosses but leaders : how to lead the way to success / John Adair.
      p. cm.
   Rev. ed. of: Not bosses but leaders / John Adair with Peter Reed. 3rd ed. 2003
   ISBN 978-0-7494-5481-4
   1. Leadership. 2. Management. I. Title.
      HD57.7.A2755 2009
      658.4'092--dc22
                                                                    2008042741

Typeset by Jean Cussons Typesetting, Diss, Norfolk
Printed and bound in India by Replika Press Pvt Ltd

THE UNIVERSITY
WINCH...

Not Bosses

But
Leaders

JOHN ADAIR is now widely regarded as the world's leading authority on leadership and leadership development. The author of 30 books on the subject, he has been named as one of the 40 people worldwide who have contributed most to the development of management thought and practice.

Educated at St Paul's School, London, John Adair has enjoyed a varied and colourful career. He served as adjutant in a Bedouin regiment in the Arab Legion, worked as a deckhand on an Arctic trawler and had a spell as an orderly in a hospital operating theatre. After Cambridge he became Senior Lecturer in Military History and Leadership Training Adviser at the Royal Military Academy, Sandhurst, before becoming the first Director of Studies at St George's House in Windsor Castle and then Associate Director of the Industrial Society. Later he became the world's first Professor in Leadership Studies at the University of Surrey. He also helped to found Europe's first Centre for Leadership Studies at the University of Exeter.

John has recently received the Lifetime Achievement in Leadership Award, and China has made him its first Honorary Professor of Leadership.

John now acts as a national and international adviser on leadership development. His recent books, published by Kogan Page, include *Not Bosses but Leaders*, *The Inspirational Leader*, *How to Grow Leaders* and *Leadership and Motivation*.

Contents

Contents

Introduction

Several months ago a young manager visited me with an unusual request. He told me that he wanted some guidelines that would enable him to lead a company with confidence. Some weeks before, on behalf of the large multinational that employed him, the young manager had approached a medium-sized company in the field in order to acquire it. But the family-owned firm decided to stay independent. Impressed by the young manager's calibre, the chairman offered him the job of chief executive. After some reflection – for the company was almost on the rocks – the young manager said yes.

'I want some kind of checklist of simple points to remind myself,' he told me. 'I know that I must lead and manage in my own way, but I want to avoid making the obvious mistakes. A few key principles – or even some rules of thumb – would be of immense help.'

Intrigued by the challenge, I suggested that we should meet four or five times and go over the ground of strategic leadership – the kind of leadership expected from someone operating at the level of a chief executive. He could then make notes on the keypoints arising from our conversations; they would serve him as the *aide-mémoire* he was seeking.

Some weeks after our meetings he telephoned to thank me for my help. He said that he had found it a help to clarify and crystallize his ideas.

He mentioned the keypoints as being especially valuable. 'They are enabling me to lead more and manage less. I don't feel now that I have to try to be the boss all the time.' After a pause he added: 'It's amazing how everyone in the company has come to life. We are beginning to surge forwards in the right direction. They are a great bunch of people.' In short, he was beginning to lead the way to success.

Sceptical that so much could have come from a series of information conversations I visited the company and met a cross-section of those who worked there. The young chief executive had not been exaggerating: the new spirit of the company was very evident and the results of that fresh sense of purpose were impressive.

What I have done here is to write in a slightly paraphrased form the substance of our conversations. I hope that you will find this book equally useful. Its message is both simple and important. Leadership matters – it matters to you. It matters at every level. Leadership at the top makes the difference.

As you will see, nothing we discussed was really peculiar or specific to industry or to the private sector. Leadership is, after all, largely an issue of people and their ability to communicate effectively with one another. It is equally important in the public sector, where senior civil or public servants may not be as concerned with profits or returns for shareholders, but where they certainly do need somehow to inspire their people to ever higher standards of service delivery through strategies for continuous improvement.

There is no one who cannot greatly improve their leadership through a little extra thought and practice, as the young manager in this book has proved. Moreover, it is such good leaders – and leaders for good – that society is now seeking. It was an outstanding General Secretary of the Trades Union Congress in Britain, Vic Feather, who gave me the title of this book when he said to me prophetically:

What industry needs now is not bosses but leaders

PART 1

Qualities of Leadership

'Tell me about leadership,' began the young manager. 'What actually is it? I have recently read two books on the subject and I am none the wiser.'

'Forget about the books,' I replied. 'Look back upon your own experience. You have been both a leader and led by others. What do you think makes a person a leader?'

The young manager looked out of the window and thought for a few minutes. 'I suppose that it's the ability to influence others to achieve a common goal.'

'That's not a bad definition, but what constitutes this uncommon ability you have just identified? Why does one person emerge as the leader in a group rather than another?'

The young manager had some ideas about that. He mentioned several qualities that he felt were significant, such as courage and perseverance. He stressed the importance of knowledge. After listening to him I suggested that it might be interesting for us both to look at the research relating to the subject of leadership.

'Not that it will tell you much that is new,' I added, 'but it may help you to put into better order what you know already – so that you can make more use of it in your own career as a manager, and – perhaps – to develop leadership in others more effectively.'

'That seems like a good idea. Where do we begin?'

'As the King of Hearts in *Alice in Wonderland* said, let's begin at the beginning and go on until we come to the end, and then stop. Consider first the most widespread assumption about leaders, namely that leaders possess certain qualities that will make them leaders in any circumstances, such as initiative, determination, patience, and so on. Not long after research into leadership had got underway some 40 years ago, some researchers had the idea of looking at the various lists of leadership qualities that were beginning to appear in the studies. They found that there was apparently little or no agreement on what the qualities of a leader are.

'When I was Adviser in Leadership Training at the Royal Military Academy, Sandhurst, for example, I reviewed all the lists of leadership qualities being taught in schools for young officer cadets throughout the Western world – the Royal Air Force, the Royal Navy, France, Germany, the US Army and the US Marine Corps among them. The only quality that appeared on all the lists was courage.'

'But surely that doesn't help much,' interjected the young manager. 'I imagine that all soldiers need the quality of physical courage, not just the officers.'

'I agree. Physical courage is really a military virtue, not a specific leadership quality. That leads us to the second drawback of the qualities approach, as I call it.'

'What's that?'

'Even if a list of leadership qualities could be identified, the qualities approach does not form the best starting point for leadership training. It is often associated with the view that leaders are born and not made. You may have heard the story of the business executive who read in his annual report "Smith is not a born leader yet." What do you suggest he should do about it?'

The young manager laughed. 'I see what you mean,' he said. 'But does that mean the qualities idea has nothing more to offer? I noticed that a few moments ago you said there was only an *apparent* lack of agreement about leadership qualities. What did you mean?'

'Well, I believe that we do know *some* things about the qualities of leaders. In the first instance, leaders should possess and exemplify the qualities expected or required in that particular working group. Physical courage, for example, may not make you into a military leader, but you cannot be one without it. You could apply the same principle to all working groups – engineers, accountants, academics, nurses, ministers, politicians…'

'And managers?'

'Of course,' I replied. 'If you want to be leader of managers – a managing director or chief executive – you should personify the qualities that are expected or required in all managers. We should have to return to the question of what they might be. But leadership is more than possessing the qualities that are required and respected in your walk of life. There are certain qualities that are the hallmarks of good leaders. Let me write down some headings on the flip chart:

▓ *Integrity*	Integrity has been defined as the quality that makes people trust you. And trust is of central importance in all personal relationships. Integrity means literally personal wholeness. It also conveys the sense of adherence to standards or values outside yourself – especially the truth. Trust and truth are first cousins.
▓ *Enthusiasm*	I cannot think of any leaders I know who lack enthusiasm, can you? It seems to be a general characteristic of leaders.
▓ *Warmth*	A 'cold fish' does not usually make a good leader. A warm personality is infectious.
▓ *Calmness*	An important characteristic, recognized long ago by the Roman historian Tacitus when he wrote: 'Reason and calm judgement, the qualities especially belonging to a leader.'
▓ *Tough but fair*	The combination of toughness – or demandingness – and fairness has emerged in industry during the past 10 years as a desirable quality.

'From the last point you can see that it's the juxtaposition of qualities – that pattern of qualities – that matters most. Just as oxygen combined with hydrogen is somewhat different from oxygen when it links up with carbon, so – for example – a sense of humour takes on a different nature if allied to one set of qualities rather than another.'

'And so it's still worth thinking about qualities. But can you develop them. How about a sense of humour?' suggested the young manager.

'Yes, all leadership qualities can be developed – some more than others – by practice and experience. Part of that process, which takes place over a lifetime, is contemplating the qualities of other leaders.

'Each new leader you meet, or perhaps an attribute that you have never quite seen before. It's like contemplating the different facets of a diamond. However, valuable though it is – especially in the longer term – the qualities approach is not the best starting point for leadership development. Research changed direction.'

Situational
Leadership

'A second main approach to the study of leadership has emphasized the importance of the *situation* in determining who should become – and remain – the leader of a group. For, according to the early situationalists, there is no such thing as a born leader; it all depends on the situation. Put a person in one situation and he or she may emerge as a leader; put him or her in another one and he or she will not. Churchill was undoubtedly a great leader in wartime, but was he so successful in peace?

'In fact in the very year in which Churchill became Prime Minister – 1940 – an American professor called W O Jenkins made a study of leadership and concluded with a classic definition of the situational approach:

Leadership is specific to the particular situation under investigation. Who becomes the leader of a particular group engaging in a particular activity and what the leadership characteristics are in the given case are a function of the specific situation... There are wide variations in the characteristics of individuals who become leaders in similar situations and even greater divergence in leadership behaviour in different situations... The only common factor appears to be that leaders in a particular field need and tend to possess superior general or technical competence or knowledge in that area. General intelligence does not seem to be the answer.

'Note that point about "superior general or technical competence or knowledge" in the particular field. There are perhaps three kinds of authority in leadership. There is the authority of position or rank, the authority of knowledge, and the authority of personality. The situational approach emphasizes that second kind of authority. As one manager put it:

Authority flows from the one who knows

'Hold on!' exclaimed the young manager. 'Hold on!' He began to tell me about people who had plenty of professional or technical qualifications – engineers, accountants and draughtsmen – who had worked in his company for many years. 'But no one – I repeat *no one*,' he said, 'regarded them as leaders. That theory must be wrong!'

'What do you mean?' I asked.

'Surely there is a more general leadership ability?' He thought for a moment and then added: 'I suppose that is what the "leadership qualities" people were seeking.'

'Yes,' I replied. 'The situational approach also seemed to lend some weight to the idea that you need not have an appointed or elected leader in a group – just let the situation decide who should be the leader! That sounded more democratic than leadership vested in one person.'

'You mean that they wanted to abolish leaders. Leadership becomes a sort of cake to be shared or a football to be passed from one player to another?' asked the young manager incredulously.

'You're right,' I answered, 'but perhaps we should not go into the way that culture and climate has influenced research into leadership at this point. As an alternative to what may seem like democratic turn-taking in leadership responsibility, we can now see that what works better is a flexibility on the part of the designated leader. Initially people may require and welcome a considerable degree of direction. Later they may simply need coaching or support. When the team is performing really well and clearly achieving its task, people may prefer to be allowed to get on with it without interference. If they encounter problems it may, once again, be appropriate for the leader to offer support or even perhaps direction if superior knowledge or experience of similar situations is helpful and the advice is therefore effective.'

Functional Leadership

'There are three ingredients or variables when people are working together: the *leader* himself or herself – personality and character – the *situation* in which it's all happening, and the *group*, the followers or subordinates,' I continued.

'The next approach to leadership stemmed from studies on the third ingredient – the group. All working groups are different from each other. Providing it has been together for some time a working group develops a *group personality*, as a British Prime Minister writing about Cabinets called it. Because of this factor, within the same organization what works in one group may not work in another. In this respect groups resemble individual persons, for we are all unique individuals with our own distinctive personalities, characters and appearances. But, you and I have *needs* in common – we shall both be tired at midnight and hungry at breakfast time. In the same way, working groups also share certain needs in common. There are three main areas of need present in working groups:

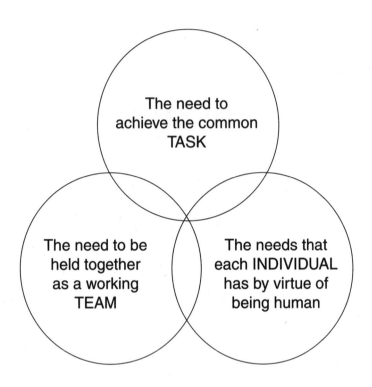

The need to achieve the common TASK

The need to be held together as a working TEAM

The needs that each INDIVIDUAL has by virtue of being human

'I have seen your three rings somewhere before,' reflected the young manager. 'But to be quite frank I have never quite understood them. I can see that a working group has a task to do, but why do you introduce this word *need*. That sounds like a bit of jargon to me.'

'Yes, I suppose that "task need" is a jargon phrase. But it is useful. It describes an important perception about groups, namely that there is a collective energy within them to accomplish what they are there to do. "The lust to finish", as John Wesley once called it.'

'And if the group is prevented from completing its task,' commented the young manager 'that drive will be frustrated. I can certainly think of some examples at work where that has happened. But what about the team circle?'

'The diagram is rather like an iceberg with most of the needs submerged below the water level,' I explained. 'The first need – the task need – is obvious to anyone. If a visitor came to your place of work, he could observe it at once. But below the surface there are these other two areas of need which are less obvious. For every group and organization exhibits potential fractures: social cracks that can widen under pressure. At Sandhurst we called it the *team*-maintenance need, because everyone knew what a team was and it sounded less like jargon than "maintaining group cohesives". Leaders have to ensure that the forces making for unity are stronger than those making for division or disintegration. If they are, then the whole will be greater than the sum of the parts. There will be some added value – or extra synergy – in the outcome of the cohesion.'

Motivation

'Tell me about the individual needs circle,' asked the young manager. 'Doesn't that somehow tie in with how you motivate people?'

'Yes indeed it does,' I said. 'Or rather I should say that it helps us to understand how people are motivated from within.'

'What do you mean?' queried the young manager.

'Well, we often think of motivating others as something we do to them externally to make them do what we want them to do...'

'Sticks and carrots?' suggested the young manager.

'Yes, but it is sometimes more subtle that threats of the sack...'

'But surely there's nothing wrong with fear as a motivator – a bit of insecurity, the fear that you might lose your job if you do not perform well, does that do any harm?' demanded the young manager quickly and firmly.

'The point I was going to make was that these external pressures on others could become manipulative, that is, when the other person is not fully aware of the processes of influence that are being deployed.'

'But don't all politicians and advertisers manipulate us?' asked the young manager, clearly thinking that I was being naive about this subject. 'What's the antidote to manipulation?'

'Apart from a basic respect for persons – a matter I want to discuss later – the remedy lies in an understanding of how people motivate themselves. It's a question of working with the grain of nature rather than against it. Let me explain one approach to individual needs.

'An American psychologist called Abraham Maslow came up with the simple theory that basic human needs are arranged in a hierarchy. These are sometimes shown in a pyramid form, as set out on page 20. Let me expound the model briefly. Maslow suggested that there is a pattern in our individual needs. Why do people work in the first place? They work because they are hungry, they are thirsty and they need somewhere to sleep. Even today, when we use money as a means of exchange, most of our salary goes in satisfying those basic *physiological* needs for ourselves and our families.

'But a satisfied need ceases to motivate. Once you have enough food and drink, once you have somewhere to sleep, other needs rise up in the human heart. You become interested in a pension, job security and safety at work. If those *security* needs are satisfied by good company policy and through social welfare, people do not then turn round and say "Thank you, we are now fully satisfied". Instead they discover other areas of need welling up within them: the *social* needs, the quality of relationships in working life; *respect* from others and *self-respect*; and then the need for *self-actualization*, a fulfilment

of personal potential by growth. The needs at the bottom of the pyramid are stronger and more basic; if they are threatened, then we jump back and defend them,' I concluded. 'The needs towards the top of the pyramid are less fundamental and less "common" in a sense. Indeed, many people in poverty never have the luxury of considering their relevance, although they can be seen as more distinctively human.'

'That's certainly interesting,' said the young manager, studying the diagram carefully. 'I can see what you mean now

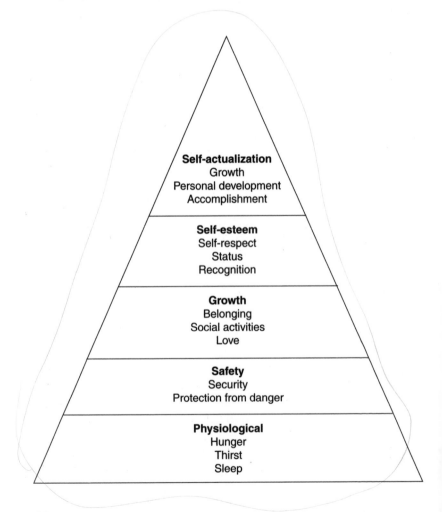

Self-actualization
Growth
Personal development
Accomplishment

Self-esteem
Self-respect
Status
Recognition

Growth
Belonging
Social activities
Love

Safety
Security
Protection from danger

Physiological
Hunger
Thirst
Sleep

about individuals being largely self-motivating. But what you say – or rather Maslow says – does raise some questions in my mind.'

'What are they?' I asked.

'First – I must be honest here – I have come across the needs pyramid before somewhere, although again I don't think I really understood it until now. But isn't it rather "old hat"? Hasn't anyone produced a later and better theory?'

'Not to my knowledge,' I replied. 'There have been other theories. Some have attracted a following for a time in the business schools but they do not add up to much. Anyway, do not fall for the "newer-is-truer" fallacy. Just because ideas have been around for some time does not mean they have lost their currency. This shouldn't be a fashion industry, although many "gurus" and their ideas have come and gone with such frequency over the past 30 years that it often seems like one!'

'But do *you* think Maslow is true?' persisted the young manager.

'No, not entirely. I look upon it as a useful sketch map of individual needs, useful not least because in my field "a picture is worth a thousand words". But it is no more than about 60 per cent true,' I said.

'Where, then, isn't it true?' asked the young manager.

'Well, first I suggest that there is no necessary progression from the "lower" to the "higher" end of the scale, as Maslow implied. It was the fond hope of the permissive society that by allowing people to meet all their needs they would progress to the "higher" end of the scale. But it is not an automatic progress. One thing doesn't invariably lead to another in this way. Not all lottery winners, for example, are as happy or fulfilled as one might assume, despite theoretically having all the means at their disposal to transport themselves to the higher strata of Maslow's model.'

'And secondly?' prompted the young manager.

'Secondly, I do not find that Maslow's liberal humanist assumptions about human nature are completely satisfying. There is surely more to life than self-actualization, as he called it. That leaves out the spirit of man, which includes the power we have to transcend ourselves. Buddhism, for example, would certainly question the basic concept that concentration on material enrichment will automatically lead to self-esteem and self-actualization.'

'And so you would discard Maslow?' asked the young manager.

'By no means,' I replied. 'The hierarchy of needs is a good introduction, but as I said, it's no more than a sketch map. Treat it as a stimulus to thought and as a guide that can take you on the first part of your journey into understanding people and it will not let you down. Shall we move on?'

'Before we do so,' said the young manager, glancing through the notes that he had taken, 'may I just check with you that I have identified the right keypoints. Some of them will be more thoughts or actions that have occurred to me as you have been talking rather than things you have said. Is that alright?'

'Of course,' I replied. 'That was the original purpose of our discussions.' The young manager then stood up and wrote with conviction on the flip chart this checklist:

Keypoints: Part 1

- Leaders should exemplify the qualities that are expected or required in their working groups.
- There is plenty of diversity in the characters and personalities of leaders, but leaders tend to be enthusiastic, energetic, calm in crises, warm, and tough but fair – to name but a few of the desirable leadership qualities.

- Knowledge – technical and professional knowledge – is an important strand in authority but it is not the whole story. Authority flows from the one who knows. A leader's knowledge includes how to adapt leadership style to the situation in which the group finds itself, and to its stage of development as a potential high-performance team.

- There is another approach to leadership, based upon an analysis of the needs present in working groups. These are:
  - to achieve the task
  - to be held together as a working unity
  - to respond to the individual needs of people.

- Individual needs help us to understand how people largely motivate themselves. The art of leadership is to work with this natural process and not against it.

- Self-actualization is not the end of the journey. The human spirit gives us the power to transcend ourselves. At its best leadership touches and releases this spirit in us.

Leadership is action not position

PART 2

The Circles Interact

Motivatioi - ish

'The three circles influence each other for good or ill in some interesting ways. If you achieve the common task, for example, that will tend to create a sense of unity and give individuals a sense of achievement. If you have a good team, you are more likely to achieve the task and the social needs of individuals will be met at a deeper level. Success will confirm and reinforce the willingness of the "followers" or team members to play their part, and to be led.'

'And if you fail in the task area?' asked the young manager.

'You can best see the effects by eclipsing the task with a shaded disc to symbolize complete failure in that area, like this:

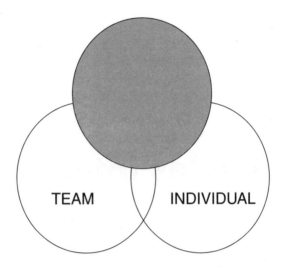

'You see that a large segment is at once removed from both the team circle – that group will tend to fall apart – and the individual circle,' I replied.

'What happens if things are adrift in the team circle?' asked the young manager.

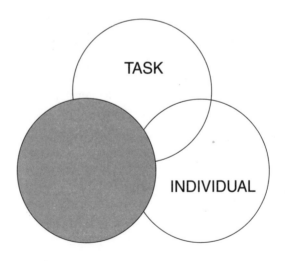

'If, for example, you have a group of individualists rather than a team, then that will obviously affect the task. And such a group will not do much to meet the individual needs of its members.' Then I added as an afterthought, 'If it's a group of individualists in conflict, your problems are compounded.'

'But that's exactly what happened at Lexton Engineering, the first company I worked for,' interjected the young manager. 'I was only there about six months before they went bankrupt, but it was an absolute nightmare. For years the senior managers spent all their time in internal politics, defending and building their own empires like feudal barons. The managing director and the finance director weren't on speaking terms – they communicated when necessary through their secretaries! The office staff looked down upon the shop-floor employees. It was like a cold war going on all the time, with occasional eruptions as frustrated people blew their top!'

'And what were the results in the other two articles?' I asked.

'The results were disastrous,' the young manager replied. 'They were so busy fighting, arguing, complaining, criticizing and politicking that they failed to notice significant changes in the market, nor did they think ahead and keep abreast with technological change. Eventually the ship sank.'

'I imagine the captain was the last to leave,' I said, trying to cheer up the young manager, who was clearly depressed by recalling the dying agonies of Lexton Engineering.

'On the contrary,' he said. 'He negotiated a large golden handshake for himself from the Board – which he had staffed with his friends as non-executive directors – just before the company went bankrupt.'

'Not a born leader yet,' I suggested. 'Still, let's look at the third set of interactions. Imagine a shaded disc over the individual circle, like this:

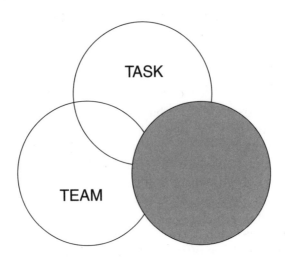

'What do you think the consequences on the other two areas would be?'

'In a way,' reflected the young manager, 'there isn't just *one* individual needs circle, is there? There is one circle for each individual in the group or organization. It's more like a bag of marbles or a pack of playing cards...'

'With some Jokers?' I suggested.

'I have met some of them,' smiled the young manager. 'But I have met even more individuals who obviously feel frustrated and underused. I notice that they tend to withdraw from the common task and also from the group.'

'You mean they retire?'

'No, no. Most people don't have that option. I mean that it's as if they *psychologically* retire on you – they take the money and wait for proper retirement.'

'An incompetent or undermotivated individual will diminish results in the task area. Such a person often contributes little to the common life of the team or organization.'

The young manager did not appear to be listening to this last point. Or at least I did not think he was. He had been jotting down some notes and then he looked out of the window.

'I like your idea of a group as being like a pack of playing cards,' he suddenly said. 'You certainly need some Aces in the team, though they can be difficult cards if they are *prima donnas*. Kings and Queens could be heads of sections or departments, or perhaps just powerful personalities in the group. The Joker is sometimes the Court Jester. Good Jokers, however, are usually catalysts for change. A Joker is a creative person in the team. Jacks are tomorrow's leaders learning their trade. Tens and Nines, even Eights are essential, but what about those Twos, Threes, Fours and Fives?'

'Well, I suppose the simple answer is that regardless of their apparent position in the hierarchy, there would be less of a team, and less coherence without them,' I said. 'The real question is, do they feel valued as essential members of the team, and as individuals? Do they add value, and is this recognized in ways that help to sustain their motivation to continue to be willing followers?'

We discussed the playing cards analogy for a few minutes until – like all analogies – it began to break down and ceased to be useful or stimulating. It was time to return to the main theme.

Leadership Functions

'In order to achieve the task and to hold the group together certain key functions have to be performed. A function is what you do, as opposed to quality, which is what you are. Let me list the main functions and comment upon them briefly:

Setting objectives   Defining or identifying the purpose, aims and objectives of an organization or group. It sounds simple but in many situations it's not easy. Objectives may need to be 'agreed' rather than simply 'set' by any one individual.

Planning   Making sure that there is a plan – agreed if possible – for achieving the objectives. You know how you are going to get from where you are now to where you want to be, and how you will know whether you are making satisfactory and timely progress.

Communicating	Explaining clearly the objectives and the plan. As a leader you should be able to answer the question 'Why are we doing it this way rather than any other?'
Organizing	Briefing, delegating, coaching, supporting, supervising and monitoring all refer to work in progress. The energy of the group should be making things happen, not fizzing off into space like steam from an inefficient steam engine.
Monitoring and evaluating	If you don't review or evaluate performance, you have no material for giving either the group or the individual accurate and helpful feedback. The aim of evaluation is to do better next time. This implies the use of measures, performance indicators and targets. As someone once famously said, 'If you can't measure it, you can't manage it.'

The young manager jotted down the functions and we talked about their applications in all three circles. He then asked if there were any functions that were specifically related to team-building.

'There are some functions – such as *setting and maintaining group standards or norms* – that do serve to hold together a group,'I said.

'Group standards?' said the young manager. 'That's another piece of jargon, isn't it?'

'Maybe,' I replied. 'But jargon is occasionally useful. Group standards is shorthand for the invisible rules and conventions that bind a group together. A more old-fashioned word that comes close to it is discipline, which of course is best if it is self-discipline – the proper subordination of an individual to the common rules, written or unwritten, of the enterprise.'

'Isn't there a danger here that groups, because they are so powerful, will enforce conformity on group members. Tremendous pressures can build up against an individual who steps out of line, can't they?' asked the young manager.

'Yes,' I said. 'You probably know the Japanese proverb that says "If a nail stands out, it will be hit on the head". Not much good if the "nail" in question is a non-conformist but essentially creative individual.'

'But the individual has to conform to some extent?' suggested the young manager.

'Of course,' I replied. 'But there should be a proper natural balance struck between the interests of the group and the interests of each individual person or, if you like, between order and anarchy. Sometimes as a leader you will have to use your greater positional power or personal influence to protect a particular individual against the pressures exerted by the group or organization. Groups can attack those they perceive to be unlike themselves, those who appear to threaten them in some way. But remember Henry Thoreau's famous words:

> *If a man does not keep pace with his companions*
> *Perhaps it is because he hears a different drummer*
> *Let him step to the music he hears*
> *However measured or far away*

The young manager stood up and walked around to the list of functions on the flip chart which I had taken off the pad and stuck up on the wall.

'Are you suggesting that a leader should perform all these functions all the time?' he asked.

'By no means,' I replied. 'Leadership is the art of knowing which of them is required and doing each function well. I discern three stages of development in that art:

Awareness	Becoming aware of the three areas of need in a group or organization; sensing their interactions.
Understanding	Knowing which function is required at a given moment or in a particular situation.
Skill	Being able to perform the function with economy and effectiveness.'

'But where do leadership qualities – you know, the qualities approach – tie in with this functional scheme of things?' demanded the young manager.

'Perhaps you can tell me,' I suggested.

'The three circles and the functions must come first,' he began slowly, feeling his way, 'because that is a kind of core job description of leadership – the responsibilities for which the leader is paid more than the team members. Qualities? Yes, EUREKA!' he shouted, 'I've got it. Qualities determine *how* you carry out functions. They colour what would otherwise be a useful but unremarkable set of "interpersonal skills". You can brief the team warmly and enthusiastically, in a cold manner in a lacklustre voice, or worse still with the impersonal one-way communication of written directives or memos. You can plan with courage and judgement or without imagination. You can direct firmly, calmly and with sensitivity or you can do it unintelligently'.

'That certainly takes us a long way down the road,' I said.

Sharing Decisions

'One thing really puzzles me,' said the young manager. 'Can't some of these functions – perhaps all of them – be done by any team member, not necessarily the leader? If the team members clubbed together and did them all, would a leader even be needed?'

'I suppose you will say,' he continued, beginning to answer his own questions, 'that in the real world, with accountability in mind – someone has to be in charge – and that someone is a leader, whatever name he or she is called by. So let me put the question differently: How far should the appointed or elected leader share the leadership functions with other members of the group?'

'It's a help here, I think, to go back to the three circles. Obviously when it comes to building up and maintaining the team or meeting individual needs everyone should pitch in – there is just too much to be done for any one person to do it all himself or herself. That is also true, of course, in all the task circle. But there is one general function or activity that stands out and needs to be looked at closely – *decision-making*. How far should the leader make or take the decisions himself or herself? Would you accept that as the key issue?'

'Indeed I would,' answered the young manager. 'For it links up with something else that has also been troubling me – where does democracy fit in with leadership? Can a team ever really be what some people have called "self-managing"?'

'Imagine a decision that can be shared in varying degrees between the leader and team members like this:

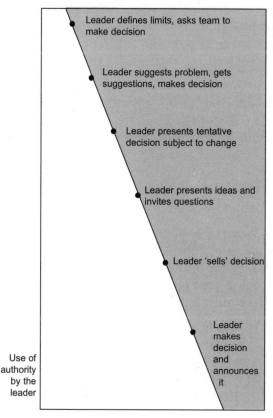

Leader defines limits, asks team to make decision

Area of authority for team members

Leader suggests problem, gets suggestions, makes decision

Leader presents tentative decision subject to change

Leader presents ideas and invites questions

Leader 'sells' decision

Leader makes decision and announces it

Use of authority by the leader

'You can see that at the bottom of the picture the leader has the largest slice of the decision, but his share gradually decreases as you go higher up the continuum.'

'And the control,' interjected the young manager.

'Yes, the more freedom you give people in a decision, the less you are in direct control of the outcome. That's why managers sometimes find it very hard to delegate when they should be doing so. But there's much to be said for making decisions as high up the continuum as possible. For the more that the team – or an individual colleague, if you are working on a one-to-one basis – shares in a decision, the greater will be their motivation to implement it.'

'Can't that be rather manipulative?' asked the young manager. 'I know some managers who make up their minds first and then pretend they haven't done so. I have been to some meetings where the manager in the chair was playing a charade.'

'The actual process itself – providing you are honest and open about it – is not manipulative. It's just plain common sense. I know all about it and you know all about it, and yet it's true for us that if your leaders take the time and make the effort to involve us in the decision-making process, we are far more likely to feel committed and give our best when it comes to making it happen.

'Desirable though it is to involve people as fully as possible in decisions that affect their working life,' I continued, 'there are some limits. Or, putting it more positively, there are four factors that play a part in judging where you should take a decision on the continuum:

The Situation	Yes, this is where the situational approach to leadership reappears in the story. Some working groups habitually operate in crises – where time is very short and where life-and-death is involved. Here the leader is expected

to make decisions quickly and the team trained to respond promptly to them. Hospital operating teams, civil airline crews and the police are three examples.'

'But these groups are not *always* in crisis situations,' interjected the young manager. 'I read somewhere that firemen only spend about one-tenth of their time actually putting out fires.'

'True. That means that leaders of such groups can achieve more participation in decision-making in such matters as duty rosters and training activities. But they must never do so in such a way that will prevent them from swinging back to issuing direct orders and getting prompt compliance. In other words, they should not unwittingly breed a false expectation that *all* decisions or *all* problems will be decided or solved by group processes.'

'That's a difficult tightrope to walk,' commented the young manager. 'I have heard the phrase "crisis management" – what does it mean?'

'Some managers lack foresight and they are lazy or incompetent in thinking and planning forwards. Such a manager has no longer-term aims and objectives, or middle-term ones either, and so he or she lurches from one crisis to another like a drunken man. "Don't worry", he or she says, "I promise it will be different next time. I must make the decision now, because we have run over the deadline, but next time it will be different. Next time I will consult you in advance. Promise." But you know what happens to "next time" – it never comes.'

'But surely you cannot plan for every eventuality – things will go wrong or the unexpected will happen,' said the young manager.

'Forward thinking should include using your imagination – trying to visualize all the things that could go wrong. You should certainly have some contingency plans, or at least a strategic reserve – even if it's only a reserve of your uncommitted time. Crises should be the exceptions rather than the rule. If that is the case, and you have prepared yourself in a general way to meet them, you can radiate calmness and confidence. You may even find time to consult people, if that is appropriate.

'Empowerment or delegation may no longer be appropriate in a crisis where the group is unsettled or uncomfortable to the point where results are severely jeopardized,' I continued. 'Support, coaching, or even significant direction and control may be appropriate. It will probably be welcomed as such by the team at such times, and it may enable them more quickly to regain their confidence, their composure, and their ability to find innovative or adaptive solutions to problems.

The Team members   The second factor is the relative knowledge, experience and motivation – the "maturity" – of the group. Clearly if your team are all recent recruits to the industry, you'll have to tell them what to do; they will expect and welcome it. If they are more knowledgeable and more experienced than you, it may be wiser – time allowing – to present them with the problem and hear their ideas before deciding yourself, or agreeing a decision with them.

'Again you have to be careful here when managers object. I remember one manager who said to me "You should see my subordinates. They are not interested in sharing decisions. They just want me to tell them what to do." I wasn't going to let him get away with that one! "What have you done to them – or rather not done – that they are in that unnatural state?" I asked. It transpired that the subordinates in question had received little or no training. There had been no attempt to communicate the firm's objectives. They were kept in the dark about the financial position. Because no one ever delegated anything to them they acquired no new experience. In fact they were thoroughly "switched off".

'And so the first rule is to have a realistic perception of the people who work with you, they are always better than you think they are – under a better leader than you or me they would really go places. Secondly, train, equip and encourage them to take their proper share in the decisions that affect their working life. That takes us on to the third and fourth factors:

The Organization	Organizations have different purposes, different values and different cultures. Where organizations place a high value on people they will tend to seek ways of involving people in decisions to ensure that these decisions are effective and implementable.
The Leader	Some leaders always make decisions at the same point on the continuum, like a needle stuck on a gramophone record. They assume that being decisive means making quick decisions by themselves, whereas it means making decisions at the right time and in the right way.'

'But I have known managers who can never bring themselves to make decisions,' said the young manager. 'They were always referring things back for further discussion or setting up yet another working party. It was very frustrating working for them. I remember coming out of one manager's office and saying, "But he *has* all the information – well, not *all*, no one has that, but sufficient – to take the decision, BUT HE WON'T DO IT". And then, of course, we started to drift and the consequences of indecision piled in upon us. Our main competitor began to beat us to the draw every time. But going back to your chart – the decision-making continuum – is there any one point on it where decisions should normally be made?'

'It obviously depends on the urgency and criticality of any given set of circumstances,' I ventured, 'but as a general rule, seeking people's ideas and encouraging them to feel involved and valued must be preferable. It is certainly, and rightly, more acceptable nowadays.'

Never tell people how to do things
Tell them what to do
And they will surprise you with their ingenuity

Styles of Leadership

'One of the many sources of confusion about leadership was the introduction of the simplistic idea of so-called "styles": autocratic or authoritarian, democratic or *laissez-faire* (or do-as-you-please) leadership. The implication, of course, was that the first was "bad" in the moral sense and the second "good". They were value judgements. Now these terms – autocratic and democratic – are political in origin. They have limited currency in the world of work. You recall our example of crisis situations. If a fire officer were rescuing your family from a blazing house, and shouting at his men to move faster, you would not say "Excuse me, I think you are being a bit authoritarian!" Research into groups at road accidents and forest fires suggests that people look for and need firm guidance from one person on what to do – they will not argue with your instructions if you seem to know what you are doing.

'In other words,' I continued, 'it is probably unhelpful – if

not simply dangerous – to suggest that one style is more "correct" (fundamentally or politically), or is appropriate for all situations, simply because there has been a general shift over the past 50 years from control and direction to the idea that modern or new leaders should be coach, mentor, teacher, and "steward of the vision". The required skill is more one of being able to use behaviour appropriate to the urgency, technical complexity or difficulty of the prevailing situation.'

The young manager didn't look entirely convinced. He had already picked up the notion of "styles of leadership" and he wasn't going to drop it easily. He pressed me with more questions about it. Finally I was happy to concede that because of this general shift in style over the past 50 years or so, there is now virtually no place for the authoritarian type of personality, who likes lording it over others (and being lorded over by others in turn – a hierarchical sort of person).

That type, now much rarer, is less acceptable by subordinates and colleagues than they would have been even 25 years ago. In that sense a more democratic style of leadership – relatively uncommon even then – has become commonplace. Style is certainly linked to decision-making but it's more a matter of personality, temperament, attitudes and values. I concluded by saying that I preferred to keep style to describe the personal way in which anyone leads. It's like your style of handwriting. Although there are recognizable styles – copperplate or italic, for example – most of us develop our own style of writing. The issue is really whether it is effective or not. A famous leader once said:

> *Leadership is the most personal thing in the world*
> *For the simple reason that it is just plain you*

'There is no one right point or "style" on the decision-making style,' I said. 'If you follow a good leader around all day, you find that he or she is making decisions at different points on the scale. Consciously or subconsciously, such a leader balances the four factors that I mentioned and comes up with the correct *process* decision – the right way to make this particular decision – 9 times out of 10. None of us gets it right every time. But the ineffective leader strikes the wrong note 5 times out of 10.'

'Or more,' added the young manager, thinking of one especially inept marketing director for whom he had once worked. 'You are putting across quite a high standard, aren't you?'

'Yes, because in order to be an effective leader you have to achieve a difficult "double". You have to be *consistent*, for people cannot abide not knowing where they are with you. That's a matter of personality and character – especially integrity and moral courage. But, when it comes to the decision-making continuum, you have to be extremely *flexible*.'

'That's not too difficult, surely?' asked the young manager.

'Not in this room as you are talking with a cup of coffee in your hand, not in theory if you like. But it's not so easy in practice. As Clausewitz, the most famous thinker on strategy, once remarked: "In war it's very difficult to do simple things". So it is with leadership.'

'It will help me if at least I can take away a summary of the keypoints we have covered as an *aide-mémoire*, the young manager said.'

Keypoints: Part 2

■ The three circles are interactive. If anything significant happens in one circle, it will have effects for good or ill in the other two areas. A leader can use the model to diagnose what needs to be done.

■ In order to achieve the task and to build the team certain key functions have to be performed such as setting objectives, planning, briefing, controlling, and evaluating.

■ All members of a group or organization should have a sense of responsibility for the Task, Team and Individual circles. But not all are accountable. That is the leader's burden and that is why he or she is usually paid more.

■ The functions are not always needed at the same time. You should develop awareness, understanding and skill so that the right function is performed in the right way at the right time, always bearing in mind the fact that actions in one area may have knock-on effects, if not equal and opposite reactions, in another.

■ Decision-making can and should be shared in varying degrees by the leader with a subordinate or the group as a whole, not least because participation tends to produce commitment.

■ In deciding the extent to which it is appropriate to involve others in decision-making on the continuum of options you should take into account four factors: the time available, the knowledge or experience of the group, the organizational culture and your own preferences or bias.

■ There is no one right style. Style depends partly upon the situation, partly upon the individuals with whom you are dealing, and partly upon your personality. A wide range of styles can be equally effective. Style is just you. When it comes to decision-making, combine consistency of character with flexibility of method.

■ Be prepared to revert from discussion to direction if necessary, if the group or team is struggling with setbacks or becoming demoralized. This will almost certainly help to maintain momentum and the cohesion of the team, restoring confidence.

Do not tell me how hard you work
Tell me how much you get done

PART 3

Leaders or
Managers?

'A big question has been forming in the back of my mind as you have been talking,' began the young manager. 'What is the difference between a leader and a manager – or are they the same?'

"What do you think?' I asked.

'I suppose a manager is accountable for all resources – money, machinery and men – and leadership is the part that deals with the human resource,' he answered.

'And so leadership is a chapter heading in the book of management?'

'Yes,' he said, 'you could put it like that.'

'That's certainly the established answer – the one taught in the business schools and on management courses. It's what philosophers call a part/whole answer: leadership is part of management.'

'Or management is part of leadership?'

'Yes, although that is suggested far less often. But you may be aware that within the past 20 years a revolution has been going on in management thinking: the part/whole answer has been called into question. Some extremists, in the throes of a reaction against management, have suggested that leadership and management are quite distinct concepts, as different from each other as chalk and cheese. You are either a manager or a leader.'

'You don't believe that, do you?' asked the young manager.

No, it is equally wrong,' I replied. 'The truth is that leadership and management are different concepts but they *overlap* very considerably.'

'Watch out!' cried the young manager, 'I know what's coming. More circles! All right, let me do it for you.' He stood up and drew two circles on the flip chart, which looked like this:

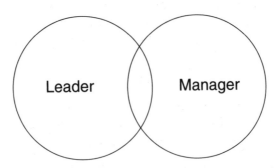

'I wasn't too sure how large I should have made the overlap,' he said. 'I suppose both leadership and management are about achieving objectives, getting results, through other people. I see you are nodding in agreement.'

'Yes, I was also reflecting that so great is the common ground between leadership and management today – for the circles have moved even more towards total eclipse in the past two or three decades – I think I would have drawn the circles even closer together.'

'What about the areas that are not covered? What is distinctive or peculiar about leadership?' asked the young manager.

Leadership and Change

'Despite overlapping so considerably,' I began, 'the concepts of leadership and management have different origins and histories, which give them a set of distinctive undertones. Even though we are not conscious of doing so, we "hear" these undertones when the words are used.'

'Surely some people don't,' said the young manager. 'I mean those who see the words as totally synonymous.'

'It is truly said that there are no synonyms in the English language,' I replied. 'Every word has its "luggage" – those associations, hidden meanings, colours and usages that always accompany it. Sometimes, in order to understand a concept – always bigger than any word – we need to unpack the luggage of several words that signpost its meaning.

'But words change their meanings, don't they?' protested the young manager.

'Yes, some words, like coins, are slowly altered by constant usage. They can be deliberately debased, too, but that's another matter.'

'Or enriched', said the young manager. 'But I am still not sure that the pure gold of leadership will mix with the iron of management,' he added with a smile.

'That's an interesting metaphor,' I said. 'Building on it, perhaps for the fusion to occur, the furnace of change has to be very hot. Leadership and change are linked. You could say that change throws up the need for leaders, and leaders tend to create change. As a friend once wrote to Thomas Jefferson:

> *These are hard times in which a genius would wish to live*
> *Great necessities call forth great leaders*

'Although a natural leader instinctively tries to change and improve things, his or her efforts will not bear much fruit unless external and internal change is effecting the organization – technological, social, economic, political and cultural change.'

'But we have seen massive changes in the past 20 years or so,' said the young manager. 'And there is no end to it in sight. The pace of change is accelerating on virtually every front. Everything is changing.'

'Not everything,' I said. 'There are constants or continuities as well as change. Change is the warp and continuity the weft in the many-coloured tapestry of history we see being woven before our eyes. But I do agree with you. Industry and commerce, and for that matter public services too, must now operate in a climate of almost constant change, stronger international competition and higher uncertainty. All that explains why the concept of leadership has once again come to the fore. Leaders like change, it's their chosen element. Managers, by contrast, have traditionally preferred to run organizations as machines. They are happiest in a "steady state" environment where nothing is rocking the boat.'

'Not much hope of that today,' commented the young manager. 'Perhaps we need to encourage all managers to accept change as a "given", and to recognize what they can do on a day-to-day basis to facilitate it in ways that everyone agrees will contribute most to the optimum benefit of the company or organization.'

Hallmarks of Leadership

'I like that picture,' I replied, 'but given the more usual background of change and continuity fighting it out like the Lion and the Unicorn, let me now spotlight some of the distinctive features in the concept of leadership:

Direction   A leader will find a way forwards. He or she will generate a sense of direction. That may involve identifying new objectives, new products or services, and new markets.

Inspiration   Leadership is linked to inspiration. The words and example of a leader kindle the motivation – the moving energy – already present in the organization, team and individual.

Building Teams	A leader tends to think naturally in terms of teams. Groups of individuals are transformed into teams. Equally, teams tend to look for leaders rather than bosses.
Example	Leadership is example. A leader will have his or her own output or direct contribution to the common task, thereby "leading from the front".
Acceptance	You can be appointed a manager, but you are not really a leader until your appointment is ratified in the hearts and minds of those who work with you.

'Management has the overtone of carrying out objectives laid down by someone else. Moreover, there is nothing in the concept of management which implies inspiration, creating teamwork when it isn't there, or setting an example. When it is the case that inspiration and teamwork exist, you may well have managers who are in effect leaders, especially if they are the source of the inspiration. But it is, I believe, unfortunately more often the case that management does not ring bells when it comes to people.'

Managing and Management

'Managing comes from the Latin words for a hand, and it originally meant handling something – a horse, a sword, a ship, a supply of money or a machine. Notice that these are all *things*. Now it is very easy to transfer the "thing mentality", as I'll call it, across the line to people. In other words, you slip easily into the habit of regarding people as things that can be "managed" like machines or money.'

'Labelled "human resources" more often than not,' said the young manager.

'Precisely,' I replied.

'But didn't the British Army introduce the concept of "Man Management" at some stage or other?'

'Yes. I once asked Field-Marshal Lord Slim if he liked the

phrase, and he almost exploded with wrath. He explained that at the turn of the 18th century the Indian Army had produced a pamphlet entitled MULE MANAGEMENT. Not to be outdone some genius in the War Office then wrote a booklet called MAN management. Later he gave me a copy of a lecture he had given to the Australian Institute of Management in which he had underlined for me the following words:

Leadership is of the spirit
Compounded of personality
And vision
Its practice is an art
Management is of the mind
More a matter of accurate calculation
Of statistics of methods
Timetables and routines
Its practice is a science
Managers are necessary
Leaders are essential

The Manager as Leader

'I notice that you often use military examples or allusions when you talk about leadership,' said the young manager. 'Weren't you in the Army for some time yourself?'

'No, I was only a National Serviceman for two years. After university I was a senior lecturer in military history at the Royal Military Academy, Sandhurst, for seven years, but as a civil servant.'

'Where you met Slim?'

'No, I actually met him later while I was Director of Studies at St George's House in Windsor Castle in 1968. He was then Governor of Windsor Castle. Why do you ask?'

'It's just that I can't get out of my head that leadership is somehow a military concept. Isn't it something that's really appropriate to the military field? You were perhaps the first to try to sell it to us in industry and commerce, and many others have developed the theme since.'

'Go on,' I said.

'As I see it, it seems to me that management is the right word in industry or commerce for all that we have been talking about, while leadership is the military word for it.'

'Not quite,' I said. 'Leadership is the "raw material": the basic functional response to the three areas of need – the three circles – in *any* working group or organization. But the *shape* it takes varies according to the field. In the military, for example, the form it assumes is called *command*; in industry and commerce, it's known as *management*; and, in the church, it's proper name is *ministry*. But the essence, the inner core, is always the three circles.'

'If that is true,' commented the young manager, 'it is a remarkable discovery.'

'It has certainly proved to be one of great practical value,' I replied.

The Roots of Management

'But I still think that leadership has military undertones,' persisted the young manager. 'Can you say some more about that?'

'Let me begin by stating what I believe is happening. In every age, it has been suggested, there is a *dominant institution* which exerts influence – not least by exporting its vocabulary – to other institutions in society. In the Middle Ages the dominant institution in Europe was the Church: hence such words as "hierarchy" (which literally means "the order of priests") and "dean". ("Dean" had actually been borrowed in turn from a previous dominant institution – the Roman Army. It derives from *decanus*, the leader of 10 soldiers – a corporal.)

'The dominant institution in the 19th century, the century

that saw the birth of management as we know it, was once again the military. It was an age of great armies. In Prussia, for example, the military influenced everything, even ladies' fashions.

'Nineteenth-century thinkers about management, like the French coal-mining engineer Henri Fayol, therefore talked much about *command* as a central activity of managing. You don't find command being taught in the business schools today!

'Now the dominant institutions of our times are Industry and Commerce. Therefore their vocabulary – words such as "manager" and "chief executive" – tend to get exported and taken on board by less dominant institutions, such as universities and schools, the churches and local government. That process was resisted in the armed forces. The battle is still being fought in the universities and schools. It has been nearly lost in central and local government and in the health service, I am afraid, where all the administrators and even some of the clinical professionals are rapidly changing their job titles to managers.'

'But you haven't yet answered my question,' protested the young manager.

'The reason why leadership has military undertones is that there has been a long tradition of military commanders seeing the essence of their job as leading men. By contrast, managers in industry and commerce have come to hold that belief – or some of them have – only in my lifetime. That was mainly due to the influence of the Second World War, where a whole generation of officers learnt their trade under some great military leaders, such as Slim, Montgomery, Eisenhower, Patton and MacArthur, and were then able to put their leadership skills to good effect in civilian life after the war.

'Actually "leader" is a general word, well over 1,000 years old, and it is found in most of the North European languages in a more-or-less identical form. It comes from the word for a *path, road* or the *course* of a ship at sea. The leader is one who accompanies you and guides you on a journey. It is not specifically a military word. Paradoxically it is "management" that is the military term. Even today the term that is used internationally for a riding school practice arena, or dressage area, is a "manège"'.

'Good heavens, I didn't know that,' said the young manager with some surprise. 'So it's management that is the military term, not leadership.'

'Yes. That is so. The fact that industry recruited most of its early managers from the ranks of engineers and accountants has given managing some of its abiding undertones, notably the strong connection with systems, machines and numbers, and also that regrettable tendency I mentioned earlier for management to see people as *things*, or "human resources", and not as persons – free and equal, intelligent, motivated and immensely capable.'

'You are implying that all the instinctive undertones of leadership are good ones and all the undertones of management are bad ones. Surely that is not so?'

'Of course not. Management implies *good administration*, the efficient and effective use of all resources, especially money. A manager is a steward. If that implication is in the concept of leadership, it is a comparatively weak signal. A less-than-good leader can be inefficient in administrative terms.'

'What else?' asked the young manager.

'The belief in system and systems,' I said. 'The concept of management as we know it today, unlike the much older concept of leadership, was born and grew to maturity in the Age of Science. Although it is going too far to say that management is a science – how could it be when its core is a response to human needs – managers should have attributes drawn from engineering science and accountancy science: an ability to install and maintain systems and an ability to administer and control finance. Neither of these distinctive undertones of management is to be found in the concept of leadership. They are essential in industry and commerce, as long as you remember that systems are only half the answer; the other half is *the people* – their quality, training and powers of leadership – who operate the system.'

'Back to leadership,' said the young manager. 'But surely the most famous generals in British history, like the Duke of Marlborough, Wellington and Montgomery, were also great administrators?'

Both Leaders and Managers

'Yes, certainly,' I replied.

'And so, in the language of today, they were leader-managers?'

'Yes, good ones.'

'Can't the "captains of industry" be *both* leaders and managers also?' he demanded.

'Of course', I said. 'It may be helpful to distinguish from each other the concepts of leader and manager, and to tease out their undertones of meaning, but I have suggested all along that they overlap very considerably. It is more a question of emphasis than anything else.'

'No, you've said more than that,' said the young manager.

'You said a little earlier that the role of leadership – the responsibility for providing the functions necessary to achieve the task, build the team and develop the individual – is the essence or core of management, command, ministry or whathave-you. The "shapes", as you called them, depend on the field in which leadership is applied. Doesn't good administration, which you seem to be saying is a positive undertone of management, really come under leadership? It implies *planning* – according to you a key leadership function – and *organizing* so that the needs of the task, team and individual will be met. Making sure that your soldiers are clothed, fed and well cared for is administration, isn't it? Can you imagine a *good* leader who is not an administrator – or manager, if you like – even though he or she may delegate much of the administration to his or her chief-of-staff and immediate subordinates?'

'I cannot,' I admitted. 'You lead me to conclude that *good* managers are invariably leaders, and *good* leaders are also managers.'

'I am happy with that,' said the young manager. 'I can see now that I am having to forge a new concept for myself out of these old words and images – it's a leader-manager concept. I want to be both. Not always at the same time, mind you. But I can see that some situations are going to call more for leadership than others – especially where change is needed. More routine activities – running an organization – require the more managerial parts of my make-up and experience.'

That conclusion struck me as true, but I could not resist pointing out that the routine option – merely keeping the show running – was becoming less common. Indeed, I can think of no organizations today that can afford to stand still. If they try to do so, they invariably find they are going backwards. Even in organizations that are not growing or moving forwards, such key functions of leadership as team-building, setting an example and developing each individual are still necessary. The young manager agreed, and continued:

'Yes, I can now begin to formulate my own concept of the leader-manager or manager-leader. But one thing troubles me. Wasn't Hitler a good leader in your definition?'

'A good leader in many respects,' I agreed. 'He was certainly inspirational and had a sense of direction. But he was not a leader for good. He was leading in the wrong direction, towards evil ends. He was a misleader. Moral values cannot be left out of leader–follower relations.'

'Let me attempt another summary,' said the young manager, standing up and going to the flip chart. 'I think these are the keypoints I shall take away:

Keypoints: Part 3

■ Leadership and management are not the same. In industry and commerce they should go together. In government we often think of political leadership and public service management, but the latter also requires high-quality leadership.

■ Leadership is about giving direction, building teams and inspiring others by example and word.

■ You can be appointed a manager but you are not a leader until your personality and character, your knowledge and your skill in performing the functions of leadership are recognized and accepted by the others involved. This is a very fundamental difference.

■ Leadership and change go together. Managing in the form of running an organization is more appropriate where there is not much change going on. When change is endemic, as it often is nowadays, managers must learn how to 'lead' it.

■ Managing entails the proper and efficient use of resources – good administration. Good leaders care about administration, the less good ones don't.

■ Management that ignores or resists change will never inspire others.

Above all else, I would like to stress our unity as a party. This was undoubtedly the biggest single factor in the final result, for the ascent of Everest, perhaps more than most human ventures, demanded a very high degree of selfless co-operation; no amount of equipment or food would have compensated for any weakness in this respect.

From *The Ascent of Everest* by John Hunt

PART 4

High-performance Teams

'Effective leadership has an end-product – the high-performance team. If you invited me to assess your leadership in a year or two, I should start by looking at your team and seeing if it has the following hallmarks:

- Clear realistic objectives
- Shared sense of purpose
- Best use of resources
- Atmosphere of openness
- Reviews progress
- Builds on experience
- Rides out storms

'Can you add to that list?' I asked.

The young manager shook his head. 'Not at the moment,' he replied. 'I was just mentally checking to see how far they described a project team that I have worked with recently.'

'Do they?' I asked.

Wearing Three Hats

'Not really,' answered the young manager. 'But there's not much I can do about it – you see, I am not the leader.'

'Hold on!' I said. 'Let's not go overboard on leadership. I have been wedded to leadership for a long time. One of the hazards of using the concept is that it implies that we are only interested in you if you are occupying a leadership role. In fact you are in three roles at work at the same time: leader, colleague and subordinate or follower (just as in private life one may be father or mother, brother or sister, husband or wife, and son or daughter).

'But surely an established leader is going to find it very difficult to work for someone else?'

'Some leaders certainly do. Montgomery, for example, scores 9 out of 10 marks as leader of the Eighth Army, but as a subordinate to Eisenhower and as a colleague to Patton – well, shall we say 5 out of 10? The ideal for any manager is that he or she should achieve 10 out of 10 in all three roles.'

'That's a tall order! I am beginning to see what it means to be a good team member or colleague. But supposing I am working for a manager who is not a very competent leader. Do you expect me to help him or her out?'

'Never expect any one person to supply all the leadership the group or organization needs. There is too much leadership required for any one person to do it all. Anyway, a leader or manager has only 50 per cent of the cards in his or her hands; the other 50 per cent are in the hands of the subordinates. Call it the Fifty-Fifty Rule.'

'But how does that tie up with something you said earlier – or perhaps I heard it elsewhere – that "there are no bad soldiers only bad officers".'

'That proverb is fairly common. Literally, it isn't true, is it? There are bad soldiers. But it's a very good maxim for officers to hold and act upon.'

'If there are bad followers – contrary to what the proverb says – that would make you select your soldiers with greater care, wouldn't it?' asked the young manager. He added: 'To quote another old saying, "Who can make a silk purse out of a sow's ear?".'

'Agreed – up to a point. Part of your leadership-by-example is paradoxically being a good colleague and subordinate. You should show a positive attitude to whoever is the tenant of the leadership role above you, as part of your loyalty to the organization. It means being the kind of subordinate you would hope to find if you were in his or her job. You may, for example, be able to complement his or her abilities or gifts. Watch out especially for any bias in the three circles – and then lean the other way.'

'It's strange that in these conversations about leadership you are suggesting to me how to be a good follower,' mused the young manager.

'And a good colleague,' I added. 'That is, when you are on an equal footing with someone else and are working together in the context of a common purpose.'

'I hadn't thought of these roles – subordinate and colleague – in such a positive way. Frankly, I regarded myself as marking time, waiting for my chance to lead.'

'You can lead now,' I replied. 'Most leadership is done from marginal positions. It is unpaid and unrecognized.'

'But it's not fair that the credit should go to some of the incompetent leaders who are supposed to be running industry,' said the young manager with some feeling.

'Who says life is fair? Someone once said you can achieve anything in life if you are willing to see the credit go to others. As they will probably take it anyway, why not give it to them?'

'And what will *that* do for my career prospects?' demanded the young manager.

'He who gives credit, gains credit. Whatever you give, you will receive back with interest. Besides, whether or not you deserve to get to the top depends on many other factors. Some people are competent to lead to one level, but at the next level up they may prove to be incompetent.'

'Levels of leadership,' said the young manager. 'Tell me more about them.'

Levels of Leadership

'The first-line or front-line leader is in charge of a small group or team. They are making the product or providing the service.'

'A chargehand or supervisor, you mean,' said the young manager.

'The names vary from industry to industry. In German and Japanese such job titles tend to have the word leader built into them. Supervisor is a Latin-based word meaning "overseer" (our word "episcopal" comes from the Greek for overseer). I wish we could find another word for it.'

'Section leader?' suggested the young manager.

'Possibly. But whatever he or she is called, the leader of the primary group has to have a high level of professional or technical knowledge and experience. Also, he or she should be a team leader, having an output of their own. When some alterations were done to our house recently I noticed that the foreman bricklayer laid bricks himself and yet found time to coordinate and direct the work of three or four other people.'

'Team-building, communicating, problem-solving and developing individuals,' added the young manager.

'Yes, all the basic responsibilities of a leader, including discipline if necessary. The leader has to take charge and be seen to be in control in a friendly but firm way.'

'Doesn't that require training?'

'Of course. I believe that no one should be appointed to a supervisor's or chargehand's job – or their equivalents – without some form of training. It's unfair to him or her, and it's unfair to the people who work for such a leader. Would you entrust your children to a bus driver who had had no training in how to drive a bus?'

'Certainly not,' said the young manager.

'Then why entrust work people to the management of those who have not been trained to be managers and leaders?'

'The middle-level of leadership is an exceptionally wide band. The essential characteristic, of course, is that the middle-level leader or manager has several leaders and teams under his or her wing. They report directly to him or her. These leaders in turn form the middle-level leaders' inner leadership team – not a bad definition of senior management, incidentally. At the more senior levels of middle management are divisional directors, for example, and all those other people who are responsible for the operations of a company.'

'How does a middle-level leader exercise leadership? Isn't he or she squeezed rather uncomfortably into a sandwich between the face-to-face leaders at the sharp end and leaders at the top, including the chief executive?'

'He or she can be so squeezed; you are quite right. One way of avoiding that happening is to take out unnecessary levels of management. Middle-level leaders can only lead if you give them the space and freedom to succeed or fail, to lead or to manage.'

'What can they do?' asked the young manager.

'Being closer to the top than the supervisor and charge-hands, they have an important part to play in the formulation of aims and objectives. Then they are responsible for implementing or executing those aims and objectives. They may not do it themselves, but they create a climate in which work groups under them can operate effectively. They make it all happen.'

'Business executives,' said the young manager.

'Yes, that's an alternative term for manager. But it takes considerable powers of leadership today to be a business executive. That takes us to another important job title – the chief executive officer, CEO or chief executive for short.'

'How does that title tie in with those other more traditional terms – managing director and chairman?'

'It is becoming a rough synonym for managing director, but it carries an undertone of having rather more power than a managing director. Those who combined the offices of managing director and chairman in their own person – not a practice I recommend – were among the first to use it outside the United States.'

'Why don't you recommend that merger?' asked the young manager.

'Well, it's the equivalent to a country appointing a dictator in time of war. It concentrates almost all the power in the hands of one person. That might be necessary for a limited time – during an emergency – but democracy has always been rightly suspicious of such concentrations of power. Remember, from your schooldays, "power tends to corrupt and absolute power tends to corrupt absolutely". The office of a chairman in a public company allows the executive leadership to be monitored on behalf of the owners, the stakeholders. Given a clear concept of the two roles, and an appropriate and effective form of leadership in both, it's an excellent system.'

'But you don't object to the title chief executive?'

'Not at all, providing it is merely a symbol of the enlarged leadership role that the managing director is now expected to play, with a wise chairman or president standing further in the background and allowing him or her to get on with it – unless things are in a mess.'

'Before we go further into chief executive's role as a leader,' said the young manager, 'can I just pin down the keypoints that we have covered so far:

Keypoints: Part 4

- Any good leader has a product – a high-performance team.

- A high-performance team has the following characteristics: clear realistic objectives, shared sense of purpose, best use of resources, atmosphere of openness, reviews progress, builds on experience and rides out storms.

- We can help to build these characteristics in the teams in which we work as team members.

- Effectiveness in the three roles of leader, subordinate and colleague – or team member – is the goal.

- Fifty per cent of the results depend on you the leader; 50 per cent depend on the quality, training and morale of those who work with you.

- Leadership exists on different levels. Because you are a good leader on one level doesn't necessarily mean that you will lead well at the next. According to the 'Peter Principle', employees in hierarchies tend to rise to the level of their incompetence.

■ The chief executive is today expected to be a leader. But many chief executives receive little or no formal training in leadership. It is the key role in any organization.

A conductor is only as good as his orchestra

PART 5

The Purpose of Industry

'We have come now to the highest level of leadership in corporate enterprise. Some people call it strategic leadership,' I said.

'Why strategic?' asked the young manager.

'The word "strategy" comes from two Greek words meaning respectively an army and a leader. In other words, it's the thinking and planning appropriate to a military general or, by analogy, to the leader of any large organization.'

'Are there any principles of strategy?'

'There are some principles of military strategy. It's up to you to see how they apply – if at all – to business. Take the chief principle – *Selection and Maintenance of the Aim* – for example. How do you think that applies?'

'You must know first why you are in business,' replied the young manager.

'Why are you in business?' I asked.

The young manager thought for several minutes. Then he got up and wrote on the flip chart: WEALTH CREATION.

'Isn't wealth something that the wealthy have?' I asked.

'No,' he replied. 'It's the wealth of nations: the money that builds the hospitals, schools and colleges. It's the money drawn from industry through taxes.'

'So industry exists to pay taxes?'

'Of course not,' said the young manager. 'Industry is there to make money. It's as simple as that.'

'Is it?' I asked. 'I know a brewery firm that could make a lot more money if it sold off all its land in the city centres to property developers. I know a farmer whose 400 acres are worth a fortune. If he sold them to a golf club he would become a multi-millionaire and could retire.'

'Why doesn't he?'

'Because he wants to make his living as a farmer. And the brewery firm I mentioned wants to make its money through producing and selling beer, or at least drink in its various forms, which they have been doing for about 200 years. I think the purpose or ultimate aim of business is to produce goods or services and market them at a profit. Do you agree with that?' The young manager nodded and then asked:

'Which comes first, then, the goods and services or the profit?'

'What a conundrum! It depends upon your perspective. Investors might stress profits. The public would probably put goods and services first. There is an analogy here with light. Scientists entertain two different theories about light: wave theory and particle theory. Both are necessary to understand light but they are also mutually exclusive. For light cannot be two different things at the same time. The best explanation seems to be that they are not actually properties of light – they are properties of our *interaction* with light. Depending on what you are looking for and how you look at it, light will reveal to you either particle-type properties or wave-type properties.'

'I see the point,' said the young manager. 'But as a practical leader it would greatly simplify things if I could have a single purpose in mind, especially as I have to communicate that to others. Which comes first – the egg or the chicken?'

'If you press me,' I replied 'I have to say that your key aim should be to produce the goods and services that society wants. A reasonable profit in the market should be the measure of your success. But don't make maximum profit your aim, with the goods or services secondary to that. That may work in the short term, but in the long term it leads to shoddy goods and poor service.

'There is some evidence to suggest that the most successful companies concentrate upon the quality of their products and services. They aim to create and keep a satisfied customer. There is considerable pride in the company in what they are doing. At the same time, they know they must be profitable. For working at a loss is like piping the fresh water from the spring down a drain. But, paradoxically, the more you give to the customer, the more you will receive from him or her. Therefore to some extent you can price according to the quality of the goods or services you are providing.

'We are now on the threshold of strategy proper,' I continued. 'You are soon going to take over as the chief executive of a small- to medium-sized company. You will be making and selling products or supplying services in a commercial way. You now have the ultimate purpose of industry fixed clearly in your mind. What will you do first?'

'I shall try to see the present position clearly and realistically. That means asking myself: "What are we actually doing now? What do we do well? What are our strengths and weaknesses?" It may not be easy to find the answers to these questions, but they strike me as essential.'

'I agree,' I said. 'The first rule in navigation is to take some bearings in order to fix your present position exactly.'

'Then I should begin the process of determining where the company ought to be within a reasonable timescale – for my company that would probably be three or four years,' continued the young manager.

'Then I must make sure that I can answer the question "How are we going to get there?" There need to be objectives and plans set and agreed for bridging the gap between the present position and the desired future.'

'Yes, that is the essence of strategic thinking,' I said. 'It's a matter of answering satisfactorily these questions:

- What business are we in – and what business should we be in?

- What advantages do we have compared with our leading competitors?

- What are our major opportunities for growth and increased profitability?

- What are the threats to our continued survival and development?

Strategic Leadership

'Let me add one important rider. What you have described – the process of strategic thinking – has to be done with others. I have noticed that top-down plans do not work. There does have to be a top-down element. As chief executive, with your leadership team of executive directors, you do have to work out a broad strategy, a set of strategic guidelines. Meanwhile, the bottom-up process of asking divisions, companies or departments to work out their own strategies within the broad framework is under way. Bottom-up and top-down strategic thinking are then merged together. That sounds rather sedate. It's more like a great river meeting the sea: an untidy but orderly process of reaching consensus.'

'What do you mean by consensus?'

'Here is a useful definition:

When the feasible courses of action have been debated thoroughly by the group and everyone is prepared to accept that in the circumstances one particular solution is the best way forward, even though it might not be every person's preferred solution.

'The most important test of a true consensus is that everyone is prepared to *act* as though the accepted solution was their preferred course of action.

'The outcome or product of this dynamic, interactive process I have described is not THE PLAN. Many senior managers have fallen into the trap of fixing their sights upon a neat watertight plan for the next, say, 10 years. That sort of blueprint type of plan is out of date as soon as it's written. Remember that planning is a leadership function; it's a continuing activity of selecting objectives, identifying alternative courses of action and choosing the right way forward within the policy framework laid down by the board of directors or their equivalents.

'It's worth reflecting on the mental qualities you require to be a strategic thinker today. I don't think you have to be intellectually brilliant or what is sometimes called clever, in order to be an effective managing director. You certainly have to be no fool, and it helps if you are bright. But brilliance is not required, thank heavens. Indeed, it may be a positive disadvantage. Napoleon once wrote to his brother Jerome: "Your letter is too brilliant. Brilliancy is not needed in war, but only accuracy, character and simplicity." And so it is in business. Strategic thinking in business is largely a matter of common sense, some knowledge, training and considerable experience.'

"Common sense sounds rather downmarket,' laughed the young manager.

'Perhaps I should have said *transcendent* common sense! Common sense is the rare power of seeing things as they are, combined with the ability to draw conclusions and take the correct action. Common sense added to knowledge and experience is the basis for good judgement.'

'I see,' said the young manager, 'that by common sense you obviously don't mean the bundle of unreflective opinions of ordinary men and women that passes for common sense. It's much more that natural capacity to reach intelligent conclusions without any sophisticated or special knowledge.'

'Yes.'

'And judgement is simply common sense tempered and refined by experience, training and maturity?'

'You have put it well,' I replied.

'How about wisdom? What is that?' he asked.

'Wisdom suggests sense and judgement far above average. I conceive wisdom to be a blend of goodness, intelligence and experience.'

'And intuition?' asked the young manager.

'Intuition is a feeling that some situation exists or is likely to exist when you have insufficient evidence for drawing that conclusion by logical reasoning. It is a valuable gift, but always remember this rule. The sooner an intuition comes to you when you are trying to make a decision or solve a problem, the longer you should take to check it out. If an intuition arrives after some time, you should be prepared to give it more immediate weight.'

'I often find that my decisions seem to make themselves,' said the young manager. 'I wake up one morning and I know what I want to do. Does that happen to others?'

'Yes. What happens is that your subconscious mind takes over and continues to work on the problem for you. In the subterranean recesses of your mind an orderly process of thought continues. Your subconscious mind digests the problem, analysing it further into parts and offering you some new synthesis of the parts. It can also evaluate for you, which is why the subconscious mind is the seat of your conscience, as your ability to discern good and bad in your own conduct is called.'

'It sounds almost like a computer,' said the young manager. 'I hadn't been aware of it in quite that way. Anyway, can we go back to strategy. Are you saying that strategic thinking is largely a matter of common sense?'

'Yes, I think so. In the first instance transcendent common sense is required to see the realities of your situation. Secondly, you need some knowledge of the available strategic ideas in your field.'

'Strategic ideas?'

'Strategic ideas are the simple ready-made formulas usually derived from studying outstanding performers. For example, the greatest military strategist was Clausewitz, who formulated most of his ideas from studying Napoleon, that natural genius in the art of war.'

'But didn't Napoleon study anyone?'

'Yes, Frederick the Great among others. All generals have some simple strategic ideas in their heads, derived from the tradition of their profession. Some of these ideas are incompatible with each other, for what works in one situation may not work in another. The best generals always think in clear and simple terms. Montgomery once asked me what I thought was the first rule of strategy. Needless to say I put the question back to him and he replied:

> The commander-in-chief must be sure that what is strategically desirable is technically possible with the resources at his disposal.

'Yes, yes,' said the young manager. 'You have to be sure that what you want to achieve is commensurate with your resources. It's no good taking over a company if you haven't got the management knowledge in that field. That's a recipe for disaster.'

'It's surprising how many companies have cooked themselves meals based on that recipe,' I commented. 'I can think of several giant corporations that were forced to spew out acquisitions because they hadn't the managers to run them or sufficient capital to develop them. "Sticking to your last" or keeping to your core businesses is a good strategic adage...'

'Unless you are a financial conglomerate,' said the young manager.

'If you are, then another set of strategic principles comes into play. For there tend to be trends and fashions for acquisitions and mergers which, before long, are often followed by reversion to the "small is beautiful" or "stick to the knitting" idea.

'As chief executive you should be the *grand chef*,' I said. 'It is your job to set the menu and get everyone else in the kitchen working in the same direction to produce the meal. If you are sensible, you will not try to do it all yourself.'

'But shouldn't a chief executive be a man or woman of vision?' asked the young manager.

'Vision is certainly a valuable leadership quality. It means literally the power to see. What the leader should see clearly is where the organization is going, or rather – since success is a journey and not a destination – in what direction it should be moving. The leader may have that vision him- or herself, or may borrow it from someone else, or the senior management team may develop and agree it through a process of consensus. But it's difficult to lead without it.'

'Impossible, I should have thought,' agreed the young

manager. 'But I sense that you are not too keen on the idea of vision?'

'That's true. Vision has undertones of poetic and prophetic inspiration. Nine times out of 10 I really do not think that it is necessary. Common sense, transcendent common sense, is what you require and that is within your grasp. Of course you need to think creatively about the future, and that may give you ideas. The seeds of the future lie in the present. But don't dress up a good commercial idea in the language of vision...'

'I must write that phrase down before I forget it,' interrupted the young manager:

The seeds of the future lie in the present

Involving Others in Strategy

'Strategic decisions are no different from other decisions, and they can be made or taken at different points on the decision-making scale. What is important is that they arise out of a proper debate over the pros and cons of the various courses of action.'

'Who should participate in the debate?' asked the young manager.

'Obviously the directors of the company. The core of them will be the executive directors – chosen from the senior managers of the company. There should also be some non-executive directors as well. The very title "director" implies a primary concern with the strategic direction of the company.'

'But most boards of directors that I know about have only

the most superficial debates about strategy,' said the young manager. 'I'm not sure what the board of directors in my last firm spent its time on, but it had absolutely no impact on what direction we were going in.'

'Some have too much impact,' I added. 'They try to run the company on a day-to-day basis, abrogating the responsibilities of the managers. That leads to the latter being frustrated and the board of directors not having time to think.'

'It's not just a question of time,' said the young manager. 'It's also a matter of having the will and the ability to step back occasionally to get the overview.'

'Absolutely,' I agreed. 'That is also an important skill. Each person at the round table has to be both a good speaker and a good listener. You have to be able to make your points clearly, simply and concisely, with a touch of humour or vividness if possible, while at the same time *listening* to, not just hearing, what the others are saying.'

'What's the difference between listening and hearing?' asked the young manager.

'Listening implies that you are genuinely open to conviction. You *want* to hear what the other person has to say and you will help him or her to articulate it. You will ask questions, for example, to elicit the meaning. It is a rare power, but an essential one for leaders. We need a listening leadership today.'

'The trouble is that directors want to be listened to, but they don't in turn listen to others.'

'Yes, I have worked several times as a consultant in organizations where groups of senior managers – those just below main board level – felt themselves disenfranchised from the strategic debate. No one listened to their views. No one seemed interested in what they had to say.'

'But they are the "engine room" of the ship, the people who

have to carry out any agreed strategy!' exclaimed the young manager.

'Of course, that is why the corporate planning process I outline above makes such sense. Achieving a bottom-up base to strategic thinking and corporate planning gives everyone a chance to contribute to the debate. As a chief executive it's your job to conduct that debate and lead it to a successful conclusion.

> The great impediment of action is in our opinion not discussion but the want of knowledge which is gained prior to action. For we have a peculiar power of thinking before we act too, whereas other men are courageous from ignorance but hesitate upon reflection.

'Those words were said by Pericles, the most famous leader of Athens, when he was speaking about the reasons why Athens was pre-eminent among the cities of ancient Greece. Should they not apply to any corporate enterprise that seeks excellence?'

'Yes, a real debate about feasible strategic options, culminating in real decisions, is absolutely essential. It has been wisely said that there is usually far too much strategic planning, far too little strategic thinking, and rarely if ever enough strategic action! As the proverb says, *An acre of performance is worth a whole world of promise.* In a moment I want to ask you about the problems of implementing strategy in an organization. But first let me try to sum up strategic thinking and planning:

Keypoints: Part 5

■ As the strategic leader of the enterprise, a chief executive must make sure that the following questions get asked and answered:

- Where have we come from?
- Where are we now?
- Where do we want to get to?
- How are we going to get there?

■ The starting point is to be clear why you are in business. Remember Cromwell's words: 'Give me the plain russet-coated captain that knows what he fights for and loves what he knows.'

■ The outcome of corporate strategic thinking should not be 'the plan' but a concept of the organization's business that provides a unifying theme and stimulus for all its activities. It guides the choice of products and markets, for example, and the types of business a company enters.

■ Strategic leadership requires mental abilities of a high order these days. Hence the programmes of graduate recruitment. But academic cleverness or mercurial brilliance are not the kind of brightness needed. It's more a question of transcendent common sense, plus knowledge and experience.

■ Don't let planning become a substitute for action. It is a leadership responsibility to oversee the process of moving from one achievement to the next.

■ Wisdom is the combination of intelligence, experience and goodness.

■ A wise chief executive will involve as many managers as possible in the debate that should always precede strategic decisions.

■ The art of listening is as important as the skills of speaking in the boardroom and in the wider councils of the enterprise. Otherwise the seeds of creative ideas will be missed.

Leadership means to me
The understanding and
Sharing of a common purpose
– Without that there can be
No effective leadership

The shortest and surest way
To live with honour
In the world
Is to be in reality
What we appear to be

PART 6

PART 3

Moving from Plans to Action

'Paralysis by analysis is a decision-maker's nightmare,' I said. 'I have known companies with large planning departments where thinking and planning ahead has become an end in itself.'

'They produce plans, not actions,' said the young manager.

'Exactly,' I replied. 'What do you think it is that makes desirable, chartered and agreed changes actually happen?'

'The fact that they are *agreed* must help a great deal,' replied the young manager. 'I wrote down as one of the first principles of leadership that *the more an individual or group shares in making a decision that affects their working lives, the more motivated they will be.*'

'Right, let us assume that your company is now agreed

upon the core purpose and its key aims. Some companies, incidentally, find it useful to write them down.'

'Is it a good idea to do that?'

'The people who benefit most from such mission statements, as they are sometimes called, are those involved in drafting them. If they are written on high and sent down the line, managers tend to file them away in their bottom drawers.'

'The aims of each section of your business now need firming up and breaking down into specific objectives for each phase of the campaign.'

'But isn't that the work of operational leaders – middle-level managers – rather than the strategic leader?'

'Yes,' I replied. 'But you should listen to their objectives and be skilled in working on them until you are satisfied with them. The first step is to ask your senior managers to write down their key objectives for the coming year and to fix a time when they can meet you in order to agree them.'

'In terms of the decision-making chart,' said the young manager, 'I shall be working towards the top end of the scale in this matter, won't I?'

'In effect you will have set certain limits. You are asking the manager to decide upon his objectives within those limits. There is plenty of time. You are dealing with a very good manager. There should be no difficulty. It helps if both of you know what are the criteria of an objective, as opposed to a general purpose, an aim or a long-term goal. The hallmarks of an objective are:

Tick box if your objective meets the criterion

Is your objective:

CLEAR	☐	REALISTIC	☐
SPECIFIC	☐	CHALLENGING	☐
MEASURABLE	☐	AGREED	☐
ATTAINABLE	☐	CONSISTENT	☐
WRITTEN	☐	WORTHWHILE	☐
TIME-BOUNDED	☐	PARTICIPATIVE	☐

Agreeing Objectives

'You can see that I have put boxes for you to tick beside each hallmark, like a checklist. When you receive each set of objectives, and are looking through them prior to your meetings, it's a good idea to check them against the list.'

'What are the kind of things that can go wrong?' asked the young manager.

'Most objectives are too vague, too open-ended. They are really aims in thin disguise. Sometimes they are no more than intentions. Objective is another of those words borrowed from the military. It means *objective point* – the ground you plan to occupy after a certain time in an attack. An objective must have a time reference and be fairly concrete in nature.'

'Granted that,' said the young manager. 'What else can I expect?'

'You will find that some managers are over-ambitious. They

set themselves and their departments too many objectives for the time and resources at their disposal.'

'Or too few?'

'Not too few, but sometimes insufficiently demanding or challenging. That brings me to you. Don't be afraid to ratchet-up these low-performance targets. In those meetings you must come across as knowledgeable, tough and fair. That will win you respect.'

'But supposing the manager involved disagrees with my suggested revision and I cannot persuade him or her?'

'Adjourn the meeting for a week. Ask the manager to go back and think about it. Let him or her sleep on it. He or she will then talk to colleagues in the division or department. His or her mind may change before you meet again.'

'You make it sound a bit like negotiation', said the young manager, dubiously.

'It *is* a form of negotiation. After all, a considerable amount of the resources of the company are entrusted to that manager. You are trying to achieve the best bargain for the whole enterprise.'

'And what is he or she after?' asked the young manager.

Relating the Parts to the Whole

'The senior executive manager – who may well be an executive director – is wearing three hats at the same time. As the head of part of the business, he or she must represent the interests and concerns of that part. And as your subordinate and as a member of the leadership team of the company as a whole, he or she should put first the interests and concerns of the whole enterprise.'

'That sounds mutually exclusive,' said the young manager.

'So it is. Just as the wave theory and the particle theory of light theoretically exclude each other and yet remain equally essential for understanding light.'

'You would have to have exceptional leaders,' reflected the young manager. 'They would have to be able to go back to their departments or divisions and present the consensus of the leadership team as if it was their own —'

'It would be their own,' I interrupted.

'Even though its consequences were dire for their people?'

'Not *their* people,' I said. 'Remember that these people work for the whole enterprise as well. As rational, intelligent and well-motivated people they are quite capable of seeing where the interests of the whole enterprise lie.'

'Yes, but their loyalty is bound up with their smaller group,' responded the young manager. 'You have repeatedly stressed the power of groups, and obviously the smaller the better. It's not as easy as you think to get people to accept radical change that affects their patch. I know because I have tried it!'

'Alfred Sloan, the former President of General Motors, once said that the fundamental issue in any organization is the relation of the parts to the whole. It seems to me that the linchpins in that interactive relation are the heads of the "parts".

'As we have noted, you will find that fashions change in organizational thinking. Once it was thought essential to be very big in size, in order to achieve economies of scale. Then the "small is beautiful" movement gathered momentum. At one time, centralization of decision-making was all the rage. Now decentralization is the order of the day, and this applies as much, if not more so, to the public sector as to the private.'

'Have you any advice to offer?' asked the young manager.

'What seems to work best is as much decentralization as possible, with some high-quality control and direction from the centre. Computers and financial management information systems allow you to know what is happening in the "parts" and if the figures demand it, you can intervene. More particularly, strategic or corporate planning in the way we have explored enables you to provide strategic direction. Finally, you have a watching brief over the process of setting objectives in the six or seven (or whatever) major parts of the business. But no more! Once the heads have received your blessing on their set of objectives they must be free to carry them out without interference from you. If they come to you for help or support, you must give it to them. They are the ones who are going to make things happen, not you.'

'I see,' said the young manager. 'But how will I know if they want support?'

'Won't they ask?'

'Some will. But others will be reluctant to ask for help. They may think it will be interpreted as a sign of weakness.'

'Well, get out of your office and visit them. Find out at first hand how things are going. A British managing director once remarked to the President of Toyota that he seemed to spend a great deal of his time out of his office. "We do not make Toyota cars in my office", replied the President with a smile.'

'Having agreed objectives, shouldn't I leave the operational leaders to get on with it? Won't it look as if I am not trusting them if I then visit their factories or offices?'

'If you don't,' I answered, 'it may appear that you lack interest. It's an option of difficulties. One safeguard of trust is to observe the principle of *respect the line*, as the military used to call it.'

'What's that?' asked the young manager.

Respecting the Line

'The concept of line-of-command, or chain-of-command, is yet another military invention. It links the commander-in-chief with the corporal. The principle of respecting the line means that a colonel does not tell a soldier what to do, he tells the major, who tells the platoon commander, who briefs the non-commissioned officers, who tells the men!'

'What happens if the colonel is walking around the unit or watching it on battle manoeuvres and he sees something he doesn't like?'

'He may be accompanied by the company or platoon commander. He will then turn to him and request that the thing is done differently.'

'Request?'

'A suggestion or request in this context is taken as an order by any sensible and well-trained subordinate.'

'And if the colonel is alone?'

'He may tell the soldier to ask his non-commissioned officer or platoon commander how it should be done; he may go back to the appropriate point in the line-of-command and reprimand someone for not passing down his orders or maintaining commonly accepted standards of excellence. Only rarely, usually where safety is at risk, will the commander-in-chief intervene himself with a direct order.'

Line and Staff

'I don't want to divert you from the subject, but I have heard that in the military a distinction is made between officers who are in the line-of-command and those who are on the staff. What does it mean?'

'That again is part of the military metaphor. In addition to line-of-command – the leaders of units ranging from sections of about 10 men to army groups of many thousands – there are staff officers responsible for performing the specialist functions in the army that are – or should be – complementary to the line. Staff officers exist at different levels. In the battalion, for example, the commander's principal staff officer is his adjutant. The intelligence officer, doctor and padre are all staff appointments.'

'No personnel officer?' asked the young manager.

'Leadership, which includes looking after the soldier',

sailor' and airman's individual needs, is quite rightly a line responsibility in units of the armed forces,' I replied. 'But there are some staff officers specializing in personnel on the general staff.'

'With two kinds of manager – sorry, officer – isn't there a danger of what you called a tension, if not downright conflict, within the team?' asked the young manager.

'That certainly happened in the British Army at the time of the Crimean War. Two reforms were introduced. First, staff officers were recruited from the line, and returned to the line when their tour of duty was completed. So the staff under-stood the problems of the line. For example, the major in the Parachute Regiment, much decorated in the Korean War, who instructed me at the officer training unit I attended during my conscript service (I take training to be a staff function) returned to command his battalion.'

He must have been an impressive teacher,' said the young manager.

'Yes, he was. Management and leadership are practical subjects. They are well taught by those who do them. They are better taught by those who have both the experience and the power to teach well.'

'What was the second reform?'

'In order to train line commanders for staff duties, a staff college was established. As only the brighter officers were chosen for staff duties (entry was conditional upon passing an examination), it also came to be seen as the school for higher command. It became increasingly difficult for an officer to rise to command anything more than a battalion if he had not "passed staff college". The next step was invariably a staff appointment. Command came later, after experience of being a staff officer.

'You can see how a good commander-in-chief would have developed an instinctive understanding of the needs and feelings of both his line commanders and his staff officers.'

'He can hold the team together,' suggested the young manager.

'Yes, there is a common vision of the army as a body with different members, each having its distinctive function and contribution to the whole. Perhaps the most important role of a military staff college is to form that vision in every officer's mind and to equip him with the knowledge necessary for him to carry out his immediate part of the drama with complete effectiveness. Perhaps postgraduate business courses such as MBA programmes try to achieve the same ends.'

'It *is* rather like a drama,' commented the young manager. 'All players have to stay in role and perform their parts according to the script —'

'Which, like a film script, is partly prepared in advance and partly written as the film proceeds,' I said. 'Or, to keep the analogy within that industry, people trained in specific roles – such as cameraman, sound mixer, or producer – can easily transfer to other films and quickly become members of a team. Everyone knows what to expect from them. It's much easier to lead a team if you have well-trained subordinates.'

'In what ways?' asked the young manager.

Two-way Communication

'Take communication in organizations, a key area for the strategic leader. From the centre to the periphery it has tended to be broadly *instructional* in nature, whereas from the periphery to the centre it tends to be *informational*. Communicating effectively in both directions requires training and discipline. The length and detail of the instructions, for example, will vary with the situation and the degree of training of the participants.'

'Can you give me an example of how it works in practice?' asked the young manager.

'The secret of the relative military success of the German Army in Russia during the Second World War was due to what they called "directive control". A veteran of that army, now a lieutenant-general, once explained it to me. "Fast forces need short orders", he said. The Russian military leaders (as their civilian counterparts do today) issued far too detailed blueprint plans. They tried to plan too far in advance. "Think ahead, don't order ahead", said the German general.'

'It sounds to me a bit like "management by objectives",' said the young manager.

'Yes, "directive control" is probably the source of what came to be called management by objectives,' I said. 'In 1944, of course, it broke down on the Russian front because Hitler began to issue detailed orders down to divisional level.'

The Roots of Morale

'I have often wondered how the German officers maintained morale on the Russian front,' mused the young manager. 'It sounds as if good leadership was the key.'

'Without good leadership, the German veteran told me, the German Army could hardly have sustained five-and-a-half years of war. As he said: "Any attempt to arouse enthusiasm for the war would have been totally misguided and no one tried this in the field. In the East the soldiers were convinced that the Soviets had to be kept a long way from German soil. There was no mutiny and few desertions. A good spirit was maintained to the bitter end. How was it done?" The German general answered his own question thus:

"It was because those in authority shared all exertions and deprivations with their men, and were exposed to every danger that might threaten. Food and accommodation were the same for all ranks.

"I have already mentioned, too, the confidence that every soldier had in the competence of his superiors and comrades. With them he felt he was in good hands and none of them would leave him in the lurch. A very important factor was this sense of security he got from being a member of his section, his platoon, his company. In the abnormal times of war, human nature gives a man a special urge to surround himself with reliable fellows and to put his trust in a leadership that will see him through danger. This was the root of the soldier's loyalty and steadfastness.

"In sum, leadership rested on mutual trust and on leaders looking after those in their charge. Caring for soldiers, in the fullest sense of that phrase, cut more ice than going by the book".'

Keypoints: Part 6

- Strategic leadership is not simply about strategic planning – that's the easy part. The difficult part is making things happen, converting vision into action.

- If your subordinates are fully involved in the decisions that affect their work, they will be committed to carrying them out. You cannot lead without winning their commitment.

- Help those that report directly to you to break down aims into clear and specific objectives. Remember to review progress at agreed intervals.

- If you will not accept anything but the best, you will be surprised at how often you get it. Tell them how it has to be.

- Try to delegate as much as possible. You will never have so much authority as when you begin to give it away.

- Get out of your office and "walk the job". But remember not to intervene directly. Information may come directly to you this way but instructions should flow down the line. That way you will not lose the trust of your managers.

■ Part of strategic leadership is building a sense of teamwork in which line managers and staff specialists, white-collar workers and shop-floor workers all feel equally valued – by you and by each other.

■ In order to lead you have to show that you are willing to live on a level with people – eating the same food, wearing the same clothes, sharing the same hardships.

It is better to light a few candles than to complain about the dark

PART 7

PART 7

Sharing and Caring

'What that German general said to you about the importance of commanders caring for their men and sharing all exertions, deprivations and dangers... could we talk about that?' asked the young manager.

'Certainly,' I agreed.

'Can you tell me if that is universally true? I mean, does it work in all armies at all times?'

'I can give you plenty of examples of all those things. Take sharing in danger. You remember that I said that commanders should personify the qualities expected or required in their men. Physical courage, the ability to manage fear when life is in danger, is one of those qualities. Soldiers would be contemptuous of any commander who chose not to share in the danger they experienced.'

'Does that apply to the commander-in-chief?' asked the young manger.

'Of course. His HQ should be within the zone of danger. But it should be far enough from the operational front to give him a perspective of the battle or campaign.'

'What about sharing in all exertions and deprivations?' asked the young manager. 'Surely that isn't necessary? Shouldn't it be a reward for being an officer that you have a more comfortable bed at night, better food and drink, and exemption from all fatigues, like digging trenches?'

'On campaign the good military leader has always deliberately shared in the deprivations and exertions of his men and encouraged or commanded his officers to do the same. Hannibal, for example, used to wrap himself in a soldier's red cloak and sleep on the ground among his men. One of Napoleon's veteran grenadiers, no stranger to the Russian winter, wrote in his memoirs: "We suffered but were proud of our sufferings, because our officers with their packs on their backs, shared our meagre rations". Wellington was furious when he found some officers in the Peninsular War not eating the same rations as their men. Slim was equally angry when in Burma he came across some officers sitting down to a meal before their men had been looked after. He also insisted on his headquarters staff having the same scanty rations as the front-line soldiers. I could go on, but I think that the point is clear.'

'Yes, I see what you mean,' he replied. 'But isn't it the responsibility of the commander-in-chief to see that there are enough rations and stores?'

'Certainly. I remember reading the diary of a soldier in the Crimean War during the 1850s who commented on the muddles of administration – one ship arrived with 3,000 left-foot boots – by accusing the higher ranks of lack of *management* – one of the early uses of that word in the English language. Good commanders-in-chief have always been both leaders and managers. But through no lack of planning or administrative foresight there are times when the "sinews of war" are in short supply. Then leaders should seek no exemption from the hardship experienced by their men.'

'You are painting a high ideal,' commented the young manager, reflectively.

'Not at all,' I replied. 'I am interested in what works.'

'But does it work in industry and commerce, in universities, hospitals and schools?'

'I don't see why not,' I replied. 'Human nature is the same, isn't it?'

'Yes, but the situation is totally different.'

'Totally?'

'You know what I mean.'

'Of course it's different. But the basic requirement to attend to the needs of individuals – the individual circle – remains constant. That means first making sure that the people who work for you get paid on time and paid a fair wage for their work. They should also have a share in any "booty" or "prize money" that's won by their corporate efforts.'

'We have just introduced a profit-sharing scheme – our equivalent to those ancient military and naval incentives,' laughed the young manager. 'I suppose you are also going to advocate single-status eating arrangements and no reserved parking lots for senior managers – all on the strength of your military analogy!'

'Not especially,' I replied. 'But I should point out that where Japanese companies have introduced these practices into America and Europe there seems to have been a positive response. Perhaps the blue-collar workers sensed some leadership at last. I know one Japanese factory in Wales where the Japanese managing director sometimes arrives even earlier than normal to help sweep the shop floor.'

'Aren't these just gimmicks?' asked the young manager.

'Not for the Japanese,' I replied. 'Let me take another example. If you work for a Japanese company and you are in hospital, you will be visited by your manager or supervisor as a matter of course, just like officers in the armed forces.'

'Isn't that the universal practice in industry and commerce?'

'No, far from it.'

'Isn't that because it would be seen as paternalistic?'

'Paternalism – or maternalism – means applying the principle of acting like a father – or mother – towards your children. It's a bad analogy for leaders if they assume that those who work for them are merely like young children whose conduct must be regulated and whose every need must be supplied by those in authority. It's a good analogy if it means that leaders should love the people that work with them as parents love their children.'

'Love?' asked the young manager incredulously.

'Love is not necessarily the same as liking, I hasten to say. Love is taking everyone's interests seriously. Love is believing in people, even if they no longer believe in themselves, and caring about what happens to them. Love is feeling warm about people, and being willing to show it.'

'Someone told me that if I looked after individuals in this way, they would all work harder,' said the young manager thoughtfully. 'To use your phrase – it works.'

'Yes, if you give to others, you will receive. But it's fatal to love people with any such ulterior motive in mind. You should do it because it is the right thing to do, regardless of consequences.'

The Case of the Injured Worker

'Not so long ago I visited a factory in England. Management had hit upon the novel idea of running leadership courses based upon the three circles for all the work force – some 800 managers, supervisors, office staff and blue-collar workers – everyone who worked there. I attended one of the courses. Over lunch one of the machine operators, who had worked for the company for 12 years, told me that he had been accidentally knocked off his motorbike outside the factory gates by one of the firm's lorries and spent nearly four months in hospital. "No one from work came to see me", he said. "There was a supervisor in the next ward having treatment but he didn't speak to me until his last day there, when he poked his head round the door to say he was going home. If I had worked in the office, the management would have checked to see if my wife had transport so she could come and see me. But no one did that for me".'

The young manager sat in silence for a minute or two, and then he said: 'I could understand it if that person had become cynical about the company and switched off at work. I had no idea that the "us" and "them" divide still existed in industry. What a lack of team spirit! Surely such class divisions into managers, staff and shop floor should be a thing of the past! Of course there must be different rates of pay, but when it comes to ensuring that a wife can visit her husband in hospital... well!'

'You don't think that would be paternalism?' I asked.

'No, that's just humanity.'

'I agree entirely,' I said. 'As the philosopher and theologian Baron Von Hügel wrote to his niece:

Caring is the greatest thing, caring matters most

The Role of Trade Union Leadership

'Can I ask you where the trade unions fit into the picture?' asked the young manager. 'Isn't it their job to care for the individual too?'

'Yes, in much of modern industry they have an important role to play. Referring back to the three circles, the trade unions exist to promote and protect the interests of the individual in relation to the interests or needs of the common task and the organization.'

'You mean that managers can't be trusted?'

'Precisely. Managers are under constant pressure to improve results. They have a tendency to think only of the task. It's a kind of bias in their make-up.'

'But sometimes that emphasis on the task is essential for the survival of the group.'

'Yes, you can see how the *task* and *team* maintenance circles get bigger and the *individual* circle smaller. In the manager's unconscious mind the three circles begin to look like a penny-farthing bicycle:

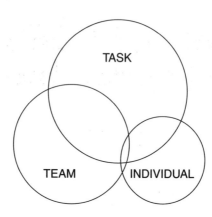

'That should be a temporary imbalance. Yes, everyone will accept that. But if you write cheques on your bank you must put more money into your account. Re-invest in the team and individual circles. A taut rope needs to be slackened from time to time if it is not to become liable to snap.'

'One essential point that I learnt in my last company,' said the young manager, 'is that the supervisor – the first-line manager – should be the one who communicates about the task. He or she should brief the team. To do that effectively the supervisor needs to understand the purpose, aims and objectives of the company. That's the framework that makes sense of the day-to-day instructions he or she communicates and thereby enables the team to achieve its tasks.'

'That's right. He or she who communicates is he or she who leads,' I said. 'It is quite wrong to allow trade unions to abrogate that leadership function. But in a leadership vacuum responsibility will always go to those who are prepared to seize and shoulder it.'

'What you have been saying is that leaders in industry – directors and managers, supervisors and foremen – should also see themselves as responsible for the individual needs circle. A leader will have a relation with each individual in his or her team as well as to the team as a whole. It's bound to be different because each individual is unique. But common to them all is a caring attitude, expressed by concern over working conditions and a willingness to listen to problems – including personal ones – and to help people to get help. Is that so?'

'That's right.'

'Won't that overlap with the role of the shop steward or trade union official?'

'Yes, but it's a healthy overlap between the responsibilities of the appointed leader and those of an elected leader. Supervisor and shop steward should see themselves as part-ners. Tension there must be in their relationship, but not neces-sarily conflict. It's also a plus for most leaders that they do not have to worry about rates of pay. Over the past 20 years the trade unions have become more like agents, negotiating pay with employers and keeping a watching brief on safety and conditions of work.'

'How about redundancies?'

Coping with Redundancy

'No one can be guaranteed a job for life in a rapidly changing society. No leader can promise that. Leaders are not themselves exempt from that law. Industry and commerce – or much of it – is essentially about taking risk. Everyone in the company – employed and shareholders – should share in the rewards of success and in the consequences of failure. There will be casualties. At least the casualties are money and jobs lost, not life and limbs.'

'But it's successful companies that sometimes declare redundancies. New technology spells fewer jobs.'

'Technological progress cannot be resisted and it's no use blaming anyone. The Luddites, who smashed machinery in the early Industrial Revolution, were expressing an understandable frustration, but we all know – even the trade unions – that they were wasting their energy.'

The young manager looked back through his notes. 'That reminds me of what you said earlier about the strong link between the concept of managing and *things* – especially machines. Perhaps management will triumph over leadership: the factory of tomorrow will consist of nothing but robots – man-like machines running other machines, presided over by a manager with a few engineers to oil the works and some accountants to count the money! But coming back to redundancies, if they are necessary, I suppose what matters is *how* they are done.'

'Apart from generous financial terms, which I take for granted, the redundancies should be made in a sensitive and humane way. That means taking time and trouble over them. If you can offer help to the person in his or her quest for another job beyond offering to write a reference – or enable him or her to retrain – so much the better. If you do those things, you can turn what might be a disaster area for leadership into something approaching a victory. I have seen it done.'

Growing Organizations

'Doubtless automation is a major factor in the decline of jobs in the manufacturing sector of the economy. We all know that. But then managers are essentially rationalizers.'

'What do you mean by rationalization?' asked the young manager.

'The testbook defines it as "the scientific organization of industry to ensure the minimum waste of labour, the standardization of production, and the consequent maintenance of prices at a constant level relative to inflation", I said. 'Not very elegant language, but there you are.'

'So jobs will get fewer and fewer?'

'Without better leadership at the top in industry and commerce that is undoubtedly the case,' I replied.

'Why does leadership make such a difference?'

'That's simple. As an American company president said:

Managers manage change but leaders manage growth

'Leaders manage growth,' mused the young manager. 'What does that mean?'

'It means that much of our unemployment is due to lack of creative thinking and entrepreneurial spirit at the top of our corporations,' I explained. 'Jobs do not grow on trees. They are the result of new products and new services.'

'How does that tie in with leadership?'

'Authority comes from "author", which in turn derives from the Latin word *augere*, to grow. An author is an originator, inventor, father or mother, one who grows things. In industry and commerce leadership is often associated more with the owner of a business – the person who created it and fostered its early growth – rather than with the manager who is brought in – I almost said bought in – to run it profitably.'

'Entrepreneurs aren't usually very good at running a business,' said the young manager.

'And their sons, grandsons and great-grandsons are often even worse. But the nexus between leadership and originating or creating something is a strong one and it can work both ways.'

'How do you mean?'

'Just as creators or entrepreneurs tend to be leaders, so leaders tend to want to grow things. They want change. If they have to cut and prune an organization down to its core businesses, they do it as a prelude to growth, to make growth possible.'

'Does that mean getting bigger?' asked the young manager. 'How does it apply, for example, to leaders in public service organizations?'

True Authority

'Not necessarily bigger. Think of growth in terms of quality as well as quantity. You can grow in excellence. Indeed, without growth in managerial excellence, sheer size will only expose you to the diseases of corporate obesity: poor communication, bureaucratic procedures and slowness on your feet.'

'Recipes for disaster,' said the young manager.

'It's curious how sometimes success breeds failure. Of course, growth cannot usually be divorced from growing bigger. This is especially so where the well-known economies of scale operate. A large hamburger chain can buy its raw materials in bulk, which reduces a key cost. A pharmaceutical company has to be big in order to fund research. And so on.'

'But – coming back to the point – you believe that if managers are leaders they will grow their business and create more jobs?' asked the young manager.

'Yes,' I replied. 'Not necessarily in the early stages. Remember that I do not see a dichotomy between leading and managing. A good leader may well have to rationalize and make people redundant. But he or she is not doing it as an end in itself. The ultimate aim remains growth. The leader will generate creative thinking among colleagues in the organization – at all levels – which will lead to expansion, new and/or improved products and services, and eventually new jobs. Therefore the leader can face difficult tactical decisions with strategic hopefulness. Furthermore, going back to your question about the public sector, it is a fact that continuous improvement of services and, what is more, benchmarking or measuring this, has become the norm in most developed countries.'

'That's a remarkably positive view,' commented the young manager.

'You can see why I always look for one key quality in a potential chief executive,' I said.

'What's that?'

'Authority. It relates to and stems from the capacity to grow an organization in adverse conditions.'

'And to grow leaders and managers?' asked the young manager.

'Leadership is self-generating. Leaders spark off other leaders – the leadership latent in us all.'

'All?'

'Yes, all of us.'

Again the young manager fell silent for a minute or two, deep in thought. Then he turned back several pages in the notes he had been taking as if he was looking for something.

'What you have just said answers something that was bothering me,' he began. 'You have stressed the importance of caring for those who work for you —'

'With you,' I interrupted.

'All right, with you. But I couldn't get out of my mind the image of paternalism, with the manager meeting the work people's needs and regulating their behaviour as if they were children. Your idea that people largely motivate themselves – they respond to their own needs as they well up within them – helps to get away from that picture. All that anyone else can do is to provide opportunity. Is that so?'

'Yes, opportunity and encouragement,' I replied.

'You see the organization as a fellowship of leaders, don't you?'

'Yes. Each person is both a leader and a colleague or team member. That goes for you, too, as the chief executive. All should have a mutual concern or care for each other. It's not a one-way traffic – that would be paternalism.'

'But how do you create that spirit if it isn't there?'

'By example. We all want to be loved. And it is easy to love those who love you. The challenge is to make the first move. Do it without expecting a response. In another time and place, possibly when you are no longer around, there *will* be a response.'

'I wish I could believe you,' said the young manager.

'Don't wait to believe. Act first, and then you will believe. If you don't make experiments in leadership you will learn nothing.'

'I have had my fingers burnt before trying to care for people,' said the young manager. 'Once I did go and visit one of my subordinates in hospital after a road accident. I arrived at the hospital within hours of it. His wife was there. As I sat with them a message arrived to say that their only daughter had been killed in another road accident in Spain. I felt like an intruder on their grief. I have never made that mistake again.'

'By never visiting anyone in hospital?'

'That's correct.'

'Timing and sensitivity are essential ingredients in caring,' I said. 'But we only learn by making mistakes. You may have had your fingers burnt, but these are honourable scars.'

'Let me record some of these points,' said the young manager.

Keypoints: Part 7

■ Leaders identify with their groups or organizations, but not at the expense of their commitment to the common task.

■ Caring for the individual should be essentially practical: it means taking seriously his or her needs and interests.

■ Class divisions and status symbols have nothing to do with true leadership. Leaders are most needed when free and equal people come together to achieve great results.

■ Leadership is a form of service. In order to lead, a leader should be willing to meet the needs of the individuals in the team.

■ Leaders may be tough and demanding but they are never ruthless or merciless – except with themselves. Showing humanity is a sign of strength.

■ Caring matters most in human relations – caring and trust.

■ A wise leader will know that he or she needs correcting on occasions. Elected representatives, such as trade union leaders, can play a positive role in promoting and protecting the interests of the individual with the three circles.

■ Leadership in the boardroom is vital if new products and services, together with new jobs, are to be generated.

Together with continuous improvement in existing products, services and processes, they are the outputs of the kind of effective leadership that really grows the business.

Your position does not give you the right to command. It only imposes upon you the duty of so living your life that others can receive your directions without being humiliated

PART 8

PART 3

Leadership and Power

'Until three or four decades ago organizations tended to be run either by dictators – usually benevolent – or by committee,' I commented. 'The emergence of a small executive group at the top is a relatively new development in the history of most organizations. That implies a chief executive now who is neither a dictator nor a committee chairman.'

'A new style of leadership,' said the young manager.

'Not really – it just takes good leadership. For the chief executive is now primarily a team leader.'

'It's a team composed of leaders,' he reflected. 'That could create problems.'

'Without repeating myself here you recall that I said how much depends upon people being 100 per cent effective in two or three roles. That is especially true of executive directors. They have leadership responsibility in their particular profit centre or function. But they are team members in the chief executive's team. And as such they are responsible with him or her for realizing the three circles in the whole organization: Achieving the Task, Building the Team, and Developing the Individual.'

'It's your idea of management as the company's leadership team,' said the young manager. 'Are the members of that senior team all equal? Haven't you left power out of the story?'

'I take it to be true that power is spread more widely now: each of us has some power,' I suggested.

'Symbolized by the one man–one vote principle in democracy,' added the young manager.

'Therefore we are caught in a dilemma over leadership. We need leaders in order to get things done, but we don't necessarily like having them.'

'Why?'

'Because we have to entrust to them – or they acquire by fair means or foul – more power per head, so to speak, than other members of the group.'

'More than the group as a whole?'

'Groups can be very powerful, especially in relation to deviant individual members. In this respect the leader's great personal power can be a useful counterpoise.'

'You mean he or she protects an individual against the group.'

'Sometimes. As I have said before, often the discordant or non-conforming individual is also the more creative one.'

'And so you are not against power?'

'By no means. It all depends on how power is acquired and the ends to which it's directed. As Sir Gordon Brunton, a former chief executive of Thomson International, said to me:

Leadership is the intelligent and sensitive use of power

Humility

'Many managers still think in a too hierarchical way; the chief executive stands on the apex of the pyramid above others. It has obviously been too much to ask you to invert the pyramid model and to see yourself as *inferior* to those around you (although in some respect or other you are inferior to everyone who works with you). I regret that I have failed to persuade you about that because it debars you from seeing leadership as a form of service, with humility as its hidden badge.'

'How did you know you hadn't convinced me?' asked the young manager curiously.

'I saw it in your eyes,' I said.

'For me the word humility has the wrong undertones. It conjures up an image of cringing self-abasement that's nothing to do with leadership.'

'I agree with you there, but look again at the word. Humility comes from *humus,* the earth. Humility means being on ground level with others. You may not see yourself as inferior to others but surely I can persuade you that you are among equals.'

'As long as I would be more equal than the others,' laughed the young manager.

'I'll accept that,' I said. 'As chief executive you should be the first among equals.'

'As long as I don't have to pretend to be a worm,' added the young manager.

'A worm lives in the earth. Therefore it is taken to symbolize humility. When a friend told Winston Churchill to remember he was a worm he replied: "Quite so, quite so, but I do believe I am a *glow* worm!".'

'At least you have persuaded me that as chief executive it would be fatal to boss about my team of executive directors. How should I conduct myself?'

'Pass them the ball. Make them look good. Let them score the goals.'

'And get the credit?'

'Why not? You can achieve anything as a chief executive if you are willing to give the credit away.'

Gaining Respect

'Shouldn't a leader keep some distance between himself and the team?' asked the young manager.

'He or she doesn't have to create it,' I replied. 'It's there already. The very fact that you are the tenant of the role of appointed or elected leader – ultimately accountable for the group or organization's results – means that you will be perceived as different. That spells a degree of psychological distance. As a leader you are never wholly part of the group: you are half in it and half not.'

'That sounds a difficult position to maintain,' said the young manager dubiously.

'Whoever said that leadership would be easy?' I said. 'Leadership is not about being popular. It is natural to want to be liked and loved, and it would be totally unnatural not to enjoy the affection of your colleagues or followers if it is there for you. But leadership is not about that. From my experience it's more to do with respect. A leader who isn't respected is hardly worth the name. Respect stems from a recognition of the leader's worth; that his or her position as leader is justly due. Respect often becomes esteem, which implies a greater warmth of feeling accompanying high evaluation.'

'Not admiration?'

'Admiring someone connotes enthusiastic, often uncritical appreciation. It's the uncritical part of that equation you should watch. You have to run the gauntlet of the group's silent appraisal of you: your personality and character, your knowledge and experience, your professional and social skills.'

'That almost answers another question I had in mind,' said the young manager.

'What was that?'

'You are stressing the importance of a leader placing himself or herself on the same level as the team. Isn't there a danger of familiarity?

'You have almost answered that question, but not quite. You don't have to be what P G Wodehouse called a "matey" person – most leaders are not – but you cannot lead people for long without constantly talking and listening to them. On a visit to North Africa during the Second World War Churchill asked Auchinleck why he did not get out of his office and visit the troops, explaining his plan to them. "Familiarity breeds contempt", replied the general. Churchill chuckled, "I find that without familiarity I cannot breed anything!".'

The young manager laughed. 'But aren't you assuming considerable self-confidence on the part of the leader?'

'That is certainly half the story. If you have what it takes to be a leader, you don't have to rely upon outward symbols – badges of rank and the like – or special privileges, such as separate dining rooms or toilets or sleeping quarters, to give you status. You already have it because of who you are and what you do. You will note that these things create distance between you and those you lead. Salary differences, incidentally, don't usually have that affect, although now the differentials are widening and becoming more public that could alter.'

'Thank heavens you are not actually against chief executives being paid more than other members of the organization,' laughed the young manager.

'No, salaries are also a principal means of recognition of the responsibilities a person bears. There has to be a proper reward for the work one is doing.'

Giving Respect

'You said that the leader's self-confidence was only half the story. What is the other half?'

'What do you think?' I asked.

'I suppose it must be the quality of the subordinates or group or whatever you like to call them. They must be the sort of people who don't take liberties.'

'Yes, in a word they should be respectful. That involves a deferential regard or esteem for you as a leader, shown in courteous attention. Other actions expressive of respect, such as politeness and the small courtesies that vary according to culture, are important. They are due to your office or role, so don't take them or their absence too personally. Remember that you are the tenant of the role. Nor should you expect them if you do not show a proper courtesy to others.'

'And if the subordinates are not respectful?'

'Then you must either distance yourself from them or find out why. Ask yourself first if you have done or said anything that is not respectable.'

'What you say is very illuminating. When I was in Japan recently I noticed in the factory, where everyone dressed the same and ate in the same place, no one was in any doubt about their place in the social order.'

'You can see how leadership becomes easier if the other people involved are natural respecters of their leaders. It is a strong theme in the Eastern tradition of leadership. There is a proverb in Vietnam which says:

> *To be without leaders*
> *To obey no one*
> *Is unworthy of man*
> *It is to behave like the animals*

'I can see that a good subordinate or follower will be deferential in the sense of having a courteous regard for the appointed or elected leader, as to someone to whom respect is due. But that word deferential sticks in my gullet. Why is that?'

'In our supposedly egalitarian society it's not exactly a popular idea. But it's the reality that counts, not the word. Even in gangs of youths you will find that there is a social order, and that one person is deferred to more than others. The danger in most groups is too much deference, not too little, and that takes us back to the boardroom.'

'What do you mean?'

'The proper respect that we have discerned can degenerate into ingratiating behaviour of one kind or another. Some people will try to get themselves into favour with you or to render themselves agreeable by deferring to everything you say.'

'How do I stop that happening?' asked the young manager.

'What do you think would be the best way?'

'I suppose I have to make it clear that agreeing with whatever I say is not the way to gain my favour. Nor must I mistake disagreement for disloyalty,' he replied.

'I cannot put it better than that. In discussions before decisions it's the truth that must lead, not you. People should submit to the better argument, not to your pronouncements. It still remains your role to persuade, to pull things together, to articulate consensus or even to decide where consensus is lacking. But you need people around you who will argue the case, disagree with you, courteously oppose you. Avoid yes-men.'

'In other words, I have to respect the knowledge, experience, skill and integrity of the executive directors and senior managers in the company's leadership team?' said the young manager.

'Respect has to be given. If you do not respect people, all people, as persons, they will soon sense it and pay you back in kind. It is essential to respect each person's freedom and to acknowledge the power that's in them. If you give people liberty, they will not take liberties. And you will never have so much authority as when you have given it to others.'

The young manager reflected for a minute or two. Once more he stood up and walked about the room. Then he sat down again. 'I am beginning to put some sort of picture – almost a vision – together in my mind,' he said. 'I can see that there is tremendous power or energy in the organization if only I can locate, release, harness and direct it. Really high-performance teams need a special kind of almost invisible leadership. I read somewhere that a good leader makes the team feel that they have achieved it all themselves.'

'You are thinking of some lines by a Chinese stateman and sage of the 6th century BCE called Lao-Tzu. He wrote:

A leader is best
When people barely know that
He exists
Not so good when
People obey and acclaim him.
Worst when they despise him.
Fail to honour people and
They fail to honour you
But of a good leader who talks little
When his work is done
His aim fulfilled
They will all say
'We did this ourselves'

Leadership and Hierarchy

'The position you hold is rather paradoxical. On the one hand you believe in some form of hierarchy in human affairs. You use words like "subordinates". You even expect them to be deferential! Yet on the other hand you seem to be advocating the opposite – a leadership that seeks no special status, no privileges, no favours. How do you square this self-effacing sort of leadership with hierarchy?'

'I can't square it with hierarchy in one sense, namely that power and wisdom are given by divine right to the person at the top of the pyramid and then pass from him – it's a very male idea – downwards to those he appoints or lays his hands upon. But hierarchy as a graded series of people presents no problems. Indeed any form of leadership would be impossible without it. But it's irrelevant to the core question: how do you get free and equal people to cooperate together in a common will. I believe that "command from above" is ineffective. What is needed is "leadership from within".'

'Before we talk about that,' said the young manager, 'let me again write down the keypoints that have emerged:

Keypoints: Part 8

- Organizations today are usually led by a small leadership team. The chief executive's job is to be the leader of that leadership team.

- Being under-powered is as bad as being over-powered. The leader should take and use the power given to him in a responsible way. He should also empower others to act and to fulfil their potential.

- Humility is becoming a key leadership quality. It means openness, the willingness to admit mistakes or errors, and the total lack of arrogance. It does not mean the absence of a proper self-confidence.

- As a manager you should expect people to respect you as the tenant of that office. But you will never gain respect unless you show respect – to your superior, your subordinates and your colleagues.

- The test of your leadership is whether or not the task is achieved. If it is, expect them all to say "we did it ourselves".

PART 9

Leadership from Within

'Leadership from within,' said the young manager. 'What did you mean by that?'

'Let's use the light analogy again. Like light, leadership can be refracted into both qualities and functions: what you are and what you do. Like the wave and particle theories of light, these two approaches may look incompatible but they are both aspects of truth. You aren't listening?'

'No, it's not that,' said the young manager. 'I do agree with you that a leader needs skills and that some of the well-known qualities – confidence, enthusiasm, moral courage – are essential. But I was trying to think more deeply about myself – whether or not I have that "leadership from within" as you called it. It's a holistic phrase, isn't it? It pulls together the threads.'

'Yes, it does.'

'Before we met I had thought my job as a chief executive would be "leadership from above". Now I am beginning to see that "leadership from within" means not separating oneself from people.'

'Spatial metaphors – above, within, in front or behind – must always be balanced against each other. The real antithesis is between being a boss and being a leader. Boss comes from the Afrikaans word *baas*, a master. Another paradox for you: if you wish to lead others you must first learn to lead yourself. As Lao-Tzu wrote:

> *He who overcomes others is powerful*
> *He who overcomes himself is strong*

'Obviously "leadership from within" does require considerable self-leadership. You must be able to control the messages that are coming out of you all the time – notably through your eyes and your tongue. Your non-verbal behaviour is often more telling because it is harder to control.'

'I have a tendency to lose my temper,' admitted the young manager.

'Controlled anger is much more effective. It's not a bad thing to have in your armoury what Josephus called "the glare of a general". Napoleon's veterans were said to be more frightened by the look in the Emperor's eye than the glinting bayonets of the enemy.'

'Back to your favourite military analogies,' said the young manager with a smile.

'Let us explore *your* favourite analogy for leadership, then – the conductor of an orchestra. Sir Thomas Beecham used the hall of my school to rehearse the Royal Philharmonic Orchestra and I used to watch him at work. Jack Brymer, the clarinettist, recently recalled that "for Beecham conducting was a silent, choreographic art. When he turned his eye on you, you knew exactly how it had to be. Most of his magic was in his eye – it wasn't in his beat".'

' "The magic was in his eye",' repeated the young manager. 'What a marvellous phrase!'

'Something else Jack Brymer said about Sir Thomas Beecham sticks in my mind: "His gestures also conveyed to the audience how it had to be. A great conductor must take the audience into a performance".'

The Leader as Conductor

'That was the trouble when his successor took over. He was a fine conductor from in front but he radiated absolutely nothing behind him and everybody missed that. Of course it was impossible to follow Tommy. If you substitute "organization" for "audience", I think you get a good picture of what a great chief executive does.'

'Is the management team the orchestra and the organization the audience?' queried the young manager.

'Taken literally that's nonsense. It's more a question of concentric circles. A much wider circle than the senior executive team should pick up the tempo, balance and spirit of the music from the chief executive. What you say, however, has triggered another idea in my mind: the conductor stands on the boundary between the producers – the musicians – and the paying customers – the audience. He has to create a harmony between them.'

'Soon you'll persuade me that the financial press are really the music critics,' laughed the young manager.

'Another famous conductor, Sir Henry Wood, was a larger-than-life character. He had colossal energy. Someone who played under him said that he had "the kind of personality you could feel if he came into a room". That's "presence". In his case it was coupled with a flamboyant nature. Once, when the London Symphony Orchestra had become almost muti-nous, he invited them all to dinner at the Langham Hotel. The trouble subsided after that.

'According to another player, Sir Henry Wood never demanded, he requested. There was never anything offensive about him. Sir John Barbirolli was always publicly critical to sections of the orchestra, such as the strings or the cellists, never to an individual. "That would be victimizing", he said. All the best conductors adopt the same manner. They are authoritative without being authoritarian.'

'You keep quoting what the musicians say about the conductors,' said the young manager.

'Yes, you may recall a point I made earlier: you can be appointed a manager – or conductor – but you are not a leader until your appointment is ratified in the hearts and minds of those who work with you. Therefore, in assessing a person's leadership why not listen to those who work under his or her baton? Usually people are very perceptive. An experi-enced orchestra can appraise a conductor new to it within minutes. Let's look at another conductor, Sir Adrian Boult. Musically he was a purist. He looked very strict and was rather irritable. Indeed he could be very angry, especially at lateness.'

'Were they frightened of him?'

'One of the violinists was asked that question and replied: "I can't say I was frightened of him – more in awe". Another member of his orchestra added: "There was never a moment when we didn't know where we were going".'

'That rings bells. Didn't we say that leadership was about giving people – a group, organization, institution, even a nation – a sense of direction?'

'We did indeed. Sir Adrian Boult also said some good things about leadership:

Our people like to be led rather than driven

We conductors all talk too much. We needn't be afraid of trusting the orchestra

The longer I live the more strongly I respect the players with who I am privileged to make music

'If a great conductor is also a leader, I can see that a special relationship develops between him and the orchestra,' said the young manager.

'Perhaps being a leader is part of his greatness,' I suggested. 'But I do agree with you about the relationship. It's a matter of mutual recognition, not unlike falling in love. "I operate in terms of love", said the American conductor Leonard Bernstein. "If it's not there – forget it – I can't make it happen. They (the musicians) are there for the love of the music".

'Perhaps the more great you are, the more this corporate love of what you are doing is there. It becomes almost like a tangible presence', I added. 'Bernstein thought that the Vienna Philharmonic Orchestra was the greatest in the world. "They do it totally out of love", he said. "In fact they divide all fees and receipts from public concerts equally between them: the second fiddle gets the same as the concert master".'

'I can see that it's important for a chief executive to stay for some time with an organization if that "special relationship" is going to develop.'

'That's another significant point, one that we have hardly touched upon. Some chief executives are like mercenaries – a few are even hired gunmen! But there is no such thing as instant leadership. It's a plant that grows.'

'What's your guidance on how long I should stay in the job?'

'Not less than 5 and not more than 10 years, with 7 years as a target,' I replied.

'It's not long to be a leader at the top.'

'You might have a second or third term in office in another organization. But the point I want to make is that you should stay long enough in an organization to see if your strategic conception works. Bernstein talks about the conductor as someone with one conception of the piece who is guiding the whole trust. That conception is not dictatorial: it stems from a knowledge of how music actually works.'

'And that knowledge is gained from study, experience as a conductor, and from the conductor's ability to hear the score and imagine the composer's intention,' said the young manager.

'Yes, notice the importance of that creative imagination or vision. In this context it's putting yourself in the place of the composer and hearing the music as he heard it.'

'For a manager it could be standing in the shoes of the founders, seeing the business as they saw it and translating it into modern terms,' said the young manager.

'I wouldn't press the analogy too far. In most organizations you do not have a dramatic script or musical score to re-create and re-transfer. If you wanted to develop the metaphor further in that direction you would have to switch from a symphony orchestra to a jazz band. There they make the music up as they go along.'

'Improvising! That doesn't sound like good management to me. You need some sort of score. Isn't the corporate plan in some sense the score of the chief executive?' asked the young manager.

'It's more your vision which arises from studying the score, or, if you prefer it, your conception of how it has to be. There are usually two routes to discovering that: by creative flair or insight on the one hand and by the application of common sense to the environment on the other.'

'Back to transcendent common sense,' commented the young manager.

'The next step outlined by Leonard Bernstein sounds equally simple. "Your task is to get the orchestra you are working with to deliver that music in your head. It's a three-stage operation: hear inwardly, get it over to the orchestra, and get them to give it to the audience".'

'Vision, communication and creating a satisfied customer.'

'Precisely. But you can see why the modern breed of conductor, jetting around the world, doesn't have time for contemplation.'

'Contemplation? Not many senior managers I know have time for that either. They are too busy. I don't intend to make that mistake, for I can see that contemplation is necessary. Let me write down the keypoints for some later reflection':

Keypoints: Part 9

■ 'Leadership from within' is more valuable than 'leadership from above'. That kind of leadership is an essential characteristic of the really effective chief executive.

- Self-leadership comes before leading others. That means setting aims and objectives for yourself as well as high standards of conduct and communication.

- A chief executive is like the conductor of a large orchestra. One key test of his leadership is that the orchestra should know where it's going and play together.

- Like a conductor, a chief executive needs 'presence', not least because he or she stands on the boundary between the organization and its environment.

- Don't talk too much. Don't be afraid of trusting the orchestra.

- People prefer to be led rather than driven.

- Look upon leadership of the people who work with you as a privilege. Bring to mind what they give to you as well as what you give to them.

Conclusion

'Is there anything else I can say that would be useful?' I asked, conscious that time was passing.

'I don't think so,' said the young manager. 'I have to go and do the job now. At least I know now what pitfalls to avoid.'

'You cannot avoid mistakes. Leadership is learnt by experience; it's a practical art. Let your colleagues and subordinates teach you.'

'But talking to you has helped. You have made me think for myself. I have profited from other people's experience. I know I still have to start at the bottom of the learning curve, but you have given me a framework and some principles that will help me on the way.'

'You aren't put off by the difficulties of leadership?'

'On the contrary, I now see them as challenges. I am much

encouraged by these words of John Buchan about people. If I can see people – and leadership – in that light, I know that I can lead the way to success:

> *The task of leadership is not to put greatness into humanity but to elicit it for the greatness is already there*

Notes and References

Page 15   Clement Attlee, 'In the Driver's Seat', *The Observer*, 18 October 1964

Page 19   A H Maslow, *Motivation and Personality*, Harper and Brothers, New York, 1954. See also *The Farther Reaches of Human Nature*, Pelican edition, 1971

Page 23   Dag Hammarskjöld writing to himself while Secretary-General of the United Nations, later published *Markings*

Page 34   Henry Thoreau

Page 37   R Tannenbaum and W H Schmidt, 'How to Choose a Leadership Pattern', *Harvard Business Review*, March– April 1958

Page 42   General George S Patton, Jnr

Page 44   Field-Marshal Viscount Slim, in an address to officer cadets at the Royal Military Academy, Sandhurst, 1952

Page 53   Abigail Adams, 1790, in a letter to Thomas Jefferson. Quoted in Warren Bennis and Burt Nanus, *Leaders*, Harper & Row, 1985

Page 58   Field Marshal Viscount Slim, in 'Leadership', a lecture given in Adelaide in 1957

Page 80   André Previn, the conductor

Page 97   Socrates

Page 126   *Letters from Baron Friedrich Von Hügel to a Niece*, ed G Greene, J M Dent, London, 1928

Page 139   Dag Hammarskjöld

Page 169   John Buchan, 'Montrose and Leadership', a lecture given at the University of St Andrews, 27 January 1930

Index